Copyright © 2024 Radu Spataru

All rights reserved

No part of this book may be reproduced, or stored in a retrieval system, or transmitted in any form or by any means, electronic, mechanical, photocopying, recording, or otherwise, without express written permission of the publisher.

ASIN (eBook): B0CW1C829X
ISBN (Paperback): 9798320598611
ISBN (Hardcover): 9798320602035
Imprint: Independently published

Cover design by: Art Painter
Library of Congress Control Number: 2018675309
Printed in the United States of America

PRACTICAL GUIDE FOR IT LEADERS, THIRD EDITION

Your Compass for Navigating the World of IT Leadership

Radu Spataru

FOREWORD

In the vast expanse of Information Technology and its applicable domain, navigating through its complexities and nuances I often feel akin to traversing uncharted territories. For years, I found myself trying to find guidance in the ever-evolving landscape of IT. It was during this quest that I had the privilege of encountering a remarkable literary companion, a book that not only met but exceeded my expectations – a practical compendium aptly titled, Practical Guide for IT Leaders.

Within the pages of this invaluable tome, authored by a distinguished figure whose expertise is renowned in the field, lies a treasure trove of wisdom awaiting eager minds. What struck me most profoundly was how the title itself encapsulated the essence of the book, serving as a beacon of clarity amidst the vast sea of information. It truly is a handbook in the purest sense – a comprehensive guide that transcends specific domains and management styles.

What sets this book apart is its universal applicability. Whether you're a novice seeking to unravel the intricacies of IT or a seasoned professional aiming to hone your leadership skills, the contents herein offer a roadmap to success. For me, the chapter Build Your Team is very helpful. From the fundamentals of Information Technology to advanced topics such as Green IT, the role of AI and its impact, every facet of the IT domain finds meticulous treatment within these pages.

One of the most commendable features of this book is its versatility. No longer do readers have to sift through volumes of text searching for relevance; instead, you can simply navigate to the chapters that align with your specific needs and aspirations. This is why I found this book practical again. Whether it's mastering the art of project management or delving into the intricacies of cybersecurity, the wealth of knowledge presented here serves as a guiding light in the pursuit of excellence. It pushes anyone curious in IT to enhance what he is looking for.

In my humble opinion, I do recommend this book highly thought. It transcends the boundaries of expertise and personal experience, offering invaluable insights that are pertinent to individuals at every rung of the IT ladder. To anyone seeking to navigate the labyrinthine corridors of Information Technology with confidence and proficiency, I recommend you embark on this enlightening journey and discover the transformative power that lies within the pages of Practical Guide for IT Leaders.

Siam Mauceny.

Responsible support IN/VAS (MEA), Orange Group

More than 25 years strategy and management experience at "C" Level in IT and Technical domain in International markets.

TABLE OF CONTENTS

Why This Book?
Who is This Book For?
Chapter 1. Your Journey as IT Leader
   1.1 Assess Current Status
   1.2 Create Your Strategy
   1.3 Create and Manage Your Strategy Execution Roadmap
   1.4 Manage Your Internal and External Processes
   1.5 Build Your Team
   1.6 Manage Technology
   1.7 Manage IT Budget
   1.8 IT Leader Roles Alignment
   1.9 Applicable Across All Management Styles
Chapter "Vs". My Vision and Values.
Chapter "C". Culture
Chapter 2. Assessment of the status – AS IS.
Chapter 3. Building Your Strategy
   3.1 Discover Business Strategy
   3.2 Build I T Strategy and Validate it.
Chapter 4. Your Strategy Execution Roadmap
Chapter 5. Manageme Internal and External Processes
   5.1 Service Level Agreements (S L As)
   5.2 Information Security
   5.3 Change Management Process
   5.4 Roadmap Process and Related Elements
   5.5 Tools for Roadmap and Task Management
   5.6 Monitoring and Support Processes
   5.7 Disaster Recovery and Business Continuity
Chapter 6. Build Your Team
   6.1 Hiring Process

6.2 Manage Continuous Learning - Hard and Soft Skills
6.3 Implement Salary Structure and Career Path.
6.4 Implement Motivational Systems
6.5 Manage properly Communication and Meetings
6.6 Retention strategies

Chapter 7. Manage Technology
7.1 Manage the Borders of I T
7.2 Have Key Technical Knowledge Inside Your Team.
7.3 Selection of Proper Architecture/Technical Solution
7.4 Monitoring Tools and Processes Are Mandatory
7.5 Reporting and B I - Manage Them Properly
7.6 Information Security
7.7 Manage IT KPIs

Chapter 8. Manage IT Budget
8.1 Budget Planning
8.2 Budget Review
8.3 IT Budget Domains
8.4 The Strategic Essence of IT Spending
8.5 Budget and day-to-day activities

Chapter 9. Project Management Methodology
9.1 What is the Waterfall methodology?
9.2 What is Agile methodology?
9.3 Which Methodology to use?

Chapter 10. Technologies Transforming the IT Landscape
10.1 Cloud Strategy
10.2 Green IT
10.3 AI Technology

Chapter 11. IT Leader Checklist (bonus chapter)
Conclusion
Abbreviations used in this book.
List of Diagrams and Tables
References
About The Author

WHY THIS BOOK?

Every day, we encounter stories of failure: numerous startup businesses collapse, and established enterprise companies fail in many cases —ranging from product launches to data protection incidents.

> "APPROXIMATELY 75% OF VENTURE-BACKED STARTUPS FAIL. THE NUMBER IS DIFFICULT TO PIN DOWN, AND SOME ESTIMATES SUGGEST IT COULD BE EVEN HIGHER."
>
> ELIZABETH POLLMAN (STUDY ABOUT REASONS OF STARTUP FAILURE)

These failures often arise from a variety of reasons: running out of cash, internal team issues, product development or business model flaws, fierce competition, a lack of market need, or changing circumstances.

Confronted with these stories, we might react by:

- Feeling fearful - "What if that happens to me?"
- Becoming overconfident - "That won't happen to me."
- Reflecting critically - "What are the common factors in these failures, and how can we identify and address our mistakes before they lead to disaster?"

It prompts us to question our actions and their effectiveness. Are we genuinely focused on making the right decisions and taking the necessary steps to progress, perform well, and rectify our mistakes?

Many failures are tied to IT projects and products, often

involving teams of various sizes. This underappreciated fact among many IT leaders prompted the creation of this book.

The primary goal of this book is outlined in detail in the following pages, but in essence - I aim to empower today's leaders and managers. By doing things right today, we pave the way for a brighter tomorrow, marked by successful teams, projects, companies, and personal lives.

A Brief Overview of My Working Experience

Over the years, I have garnered extensive experience across various IT domains, including administration, database management, and support engineering. My career has been a journey of continual growth and a deep-seated desire to drive positive change.

Transitioning from an expert to roles such as Team Leader, IT Manager, Project Manager, and eventually CIO (Chief Information Officer) / CTO (Chief Technical Officer), each new position brought not only better remuneration and conditions but also new challenges. This evolution required a fundamental shift in mindset; expertise in processes was no longer sufficient. New management responsibilities beckoned, including budgeting, leading teams, resolving conflicts, and more.

Despite having a job description, I sought a comprehensive understanding of my responsibilities. How could I contribute to the company's improvement and stability? How could I lead a motivated team that recognized their role in the broader business strategy beyond their individual tasks?

With nearly two decades of experience in Technology Management, I felt compelled to distill the insights I've gathered into clear, actionable guidance for others. This book is designed to be a valuable resource for any IT Leader, offering a solid foundation for mastering the complexities of their roles and driving toward excellence and team success.

I trust that this book will prove invaluable in guiding you through the complexities of Technology Management. When I embarked on my journey years ago, I yearned for a comprehensive list of elements that could serve as a reliable guide, ensuring that no crucial aspect was overlooked.

Building a foundation rooted in practical experience is essential, and that is precisely what I aim to provide.

WHO IS THIS BOOK FOR?

This book is crafted for a diverse audience, regardless of their current role within the IT sphere.
Throughout this book, I use the term "IT Leader" interchangeably with IT Team Leader, IT Manager, IT Leader, IT Director, Head of IT, CIO, or IT Projects Manager and CTO (in some scenarios). The use of "IT Leader" in this book is meant to broadly encompass these varied positions.
Stepping into the role of an IT Leader introduces distinct challenges, shaped by the specific circumstances you encounter:

- **New Company, New IT Team:** Perhaps you're joining as a new member of the IT team within a newly established company, or you might be the very first IT employee there! Key questions emerge: Where do I start? How do I lay a solid foundation for the IT team and/or department?
- **Company Growth, Expanded IT Needs:** In a company that's scaling up, the once small and efficient IT team now needs to expand. This growth phase demands careful planning, team development, establishment of rules and processes, delegation, and effective leadership, regardless of whether you already have a team with the necessary expertise.
- **Transitioning as an Incoming IT Leader:** Taking over from a previous IT Leader, whether promoted

internally or hired externally, presents its unique set of challenges. You might inherit valuable resources and insights, or you might be starting from scratch.

No matter the scenario, a common necessity exists — the need for a clear starting point and a defined destination. This book aims to provide you with the initial directions, offering insights and strategies to commence your role as an IT Leader successfully, establish and manage a resilient IT team, and create an IT environment that benefits both the company and its individuals.

Additionally, this book offers valuable insights:
- For seasoned IT Leaders looking for a new perspective on evaluating their responsibilities.
- For IT professionals aiming to rise to (or gain a better understanding of) the roles of Chief Information Officers (CIOs) or Heads of IT departments.

Regardless of your current role, your situation within the company, or the state of the company itself, this book is designed to guide you through your journey, serving as a comprehensive navigator and handbook for becoming a successful IT Leader.

CHAPTER 1. YOUR JOURNEY AS IT LEADER

This chapter provides a summary of the topics we will cover in this book. In each subsequent chapter, we will delve deeper into each subject and explore real-life cases. Throughout the book, you'll find various templates that can be used immediately.

In the preceding section, various scenarios were outlined to illustrate the diverse situations in which one might assume the role of an IT Leader. While these situations are not exhaustive, the following steps are imperative for any IT Leader to establish a robust foundation and secure sustained support from the business and toward the business.

These constitute the practical fundamental principles for every manager overseeing IT (each step outlined here will be comprehensively explained in the upcoming chapters).

> "TODAY'S IT LEADERS NEED TO BE BUSINESS LEADERS FIRST, WITH A STRONG UNDERSTANDING OF THE ORGANIZATION'S STRATEGIC GOALS, MARKET CONTEXT, AND BUSINESS PROCESSES." JILL DYCHE

Real-life story: starting position of Technology Director in a new company.

I assumed the role of leading the Technical Department in a dynamic company, responsible for delivering and managing software products as part of our business. Despite the team's size not being extensive, the company's success depended entirely on the Technical Department's delivery, quality, and overall efficiency.

Upon my arrival, after a short time, I noticed the following difficult situation: the teams were trapped in repetitive cycles, tackling Roadmap projects sequentially, resolving incidents, and attempting optimizations without substantial success. Senior developers were often split between incident resolution and projects lacking clear formalization, leading to persistent rework.

The consequences were impacting the whole company: a decline in SLA (Service Level Agreement), incidents with long solution time, and stormy dissatisfaction on the Business side. Business projects, too, were adversely impacted by the focus on incidents, generating additional discontent.

This loop resembled a dead end, where individual tasks were completed, but overall dissatisfaction prevailed, reflecting poorly on the company's results.

Adding complexity, the evolving technology landscape demanded teams to explore new trends and adopt the latest, optimized, secure, and stable solutions—something that was not happening.

As a result, the overall satisfaction within the development teams remained low.

You may be saying - "this is a normal situation in many companies", "what is exactly the issue", or maybe the issue is "too many tasks or projects" …

I would say Yes - this is considered "normal" in many companies, and I would say NO - this is not a normal situation in a company that wants to be successful.

The issue is not linked to the number of projects or tasks, even so, this part left uncontrolled may partially lead to such cases.

The same situation arose when I spoke with people. Many of them saw this as normal. In discussions about issues like incidents, prolonged delivery times, business dissatisfaction, or the lack of new technology adoption, the responses ranged from "we have no time for this now" to blaming others with "we can't deliver on time because something wasn't delivered to us," or "another department or team doesn't understand our challenges, which is why we have so many incidents." Another frequent complaint was about meetings; there were too many, preventing focus on work and leading to scattered efforts, directly impacting results.

Anyone reading this book can likely recall similar scenarios.

Now, let's examine what I did and the outcomes that followed.

My targets given by the CEO were to primarily focus on enhancing the engagement of technical teams, optimizing the implementation of Roadmap projects, minimizing incidents, and improving SLA stability.

Based on my previous experience, when addressing critical issues or starting new initiatives, I conducted a thorough assessment of the scope - to understand our current situation!

To gain a comprehensive understanding and to adopt a holistic perspective, I initiated a series of meetings with all stakeholders, both business and technical. To provide more detail:
- **With Technical Teams:** Engagements involved deep dives into their workflow, bug analysis, deployment frequency, architecture choices, tool utilization, and much more. Discussions were not limited to key technical personnel but included the entire team, either in group settings or through one-on-one meetings for critical case discussions.
- **With Business Stakeholders:** We explored their processes, gathered their expectations from the technical side, and understood their targets and the nuances of these goals.

Following several rounds of meetings and exchanges of information, I compiled a "Current Situation Analysis" as Point "A" and outlined the Targets as Point "B."
Then, the role of "navigator" began - charting the course from Point "A" to Point "B."
- If product quality was the issue, a dedicated workflow to enhance quality was established.
- If the challenge lay in project delivery, a follow-

up process was initiated on one of the projects to closely examine the real-world functioning of the project process.

An action plan aimed at addressing the identified issues and enhancing the overall situation was then developed. This plan received consensus from both the team and business departments to commence implementation.
It's crucial to recognize that solving any issue requires a view of the entire process. Technical delivery improvements alone are insufficient without addressing the project requirements, testing, or launch strategy.

Here are the actions we initiated:
- **Focus on Product Quality:** This included enhancing product quality, addressing incidents, improving SLAs, adopting new technologies, and increasing team engagement:
    - **Incident Root Cause Analysis:** Key individuals prioritized understanding the root causes of incidents, dedicating time to discussions, log analysis, and action plans for testing in controlled environments. In the event of an incident, a collaborative effort was made to collect all necessary information for a thorough investigation.
    - **Proactive Technology Exploration:** Essential for staying abreast of new technologies, libraries, and versions. Each team leader designated an individual to spend half a day each week on R&D activities related to our technology stack. This was integrated into the regular schedule, with findings shared and assessed for applicability.
    - **Addressing Meeting Overload:** To mitigate

the impact of excessive meetings, especially on longer tasks, a "no meetings day" was introduced, initially on a trial basis, later adopted permanently due to its effectiveness.
- **Roadmap Delivery Enhancements:** Improvements were made to both project and technical fix delivery processes to enhance efficiency:
  - **Unified Roadmap Creation:** A merged Business and Technical Roadmap provided a clear overview of project ownership, priorities, and resources, streamlining project management.
  - **Refined Project Initiation Rules:** Premature project starts were curbed by ensuring thorough initial specification analysis and clarity, leading to better resource allocation and minimized rework.

Guiding Principles for Action Planning were:
1. **Persistent Commitment to Quality:** Quality remains our paramount concern and is non-negotiable.
2. **Continuous Learning and Technological Advancement:** Keeping abreast of new technologies involves everyone in the organization.
3. **Unified Roadmap:** Projects are not divided into business and technical; all efforts towards product excellence are consolidated.
4. **Clarity Before Start:** Clear expectations ensure projects begin with well-defined objectives.

These approaches, part of our broader vision, values, and strategy, will be discussed in subsequent chapters.

The implementation of these processes was monitored over three months, emphasizing the importance of maintaining focus on key elements without being sidetracked by other priorities. This focus is a crucial aspect of IT leadership, necessitating collaboration with business stakeholders to underscore the importance of addressing critical issues promptly to ensure future work benefits from the solutions developed.

These were key results and takeaways (per domain):
1. **Quality Improvement:**
    - Systematic approach to addressing incidents, including architectural changes, and improved communication between technical and IT teams, resulted in a significant reduction in incidents after 3 months.
    - Implementation of additional metrics in the monitoring to detect warnings at an early stage helped prevent incidents.
    - Improvements in products and architecture were leveraged to enhance the quality of new products from launch.
2. **Peoples' Engagement:**
    - Encouraging continuous learning and the exploration of new technologies increased employee engagement and satisfaction.
    - Employees dedicated working time to learning, leading to heightened motivation as they witnessed personal and professional growth.
3. **Roadmap Delivery Enhancement:**
    - Initial challenges in roadmap delivery were overcome by changing the treatment of specifications, ensuring that work commenced only when requirements were fully specified and understood by both business and technical teams.

- Iterative meetings and discussions resulted in a clear agreement on resource allocation, leading to more effective planning and reduced delays.
- Improved specification clarity and comprehensive answers to questions contributed to easier planning of resources and reduced the need for re-work, consequently enhancing product quality and therefore faster delivery.

An important aspect to highlight is that despite achieving the desired improvements, our efforts did not cease. Should we revert to previous work methodologies, the same issues would inevitably resurface.

In the subsequent period, we engaged in monthly reviews of our results, continually striving to enhance our work processes. The more improvements we implemented, the less stressful the work environment became, allowing team members to focus more on delivery and quality rather than on resolving recurring issues.

~~end of story~~

Constantly striving for efficiency is essential.

Efficiency underpins much of IT work, necessitating a mindset geared towards identifying and overcoming obstacles. This approach must become ingrained in our daily operations: it's not enough to merely be open to change - as IT Leaders, we must actively lead and drive it.

Without this proactive stance, much of the team's effort risks being wasted, akin to the scenario depicted in the accompanying image.

Picture 1: We are too busy ... to improve.

Let's begin now to delve into an overview of the roles and responsibilities of an IT Leader.

"Your journey has just begun".

1.1 ASSESS CURRENT STATUS

Understanding your present situation is similar to locating your GPS position. Neglecting to carefully evaluate where you stand today can lead to deviations in both strategy and implementation.

I am comparing the work of an IT Leader to a journey because there are many similarities. Let's explore these.

Everyone has experienced traveling from point A to point B: from home to school, from the office to the shop, and then back home, among others.

This seems straightforward when all destinations are nearby—your home is close to your school, office, or shop. However, in reality, these places are often far apart.

Thus, to get from home to the office, we need to know when we will arrive. For this, we must first know our starting point. It sounds simple, but in truth, this is a crucial aspect of beginning our journey. At your starting point (point A), you may have your car, or you might use a bicycle with dedicated lanes for cyclists, or there may be a bus or metro station available. Without determining your starting point, you cannot be sure if you can reach your destination (point B) on time and with the resources you have.

In the same way, as an IT Leader, if you do not know exactly where your team or department stands today, planning and reaching your future goals for a sustainable, efficient, and innovative IT department becomes almost impossible.

For guidance in this critical assessment, the IT assessment template presented in **Chapter 2** (Table 1) can be a valuable tool. The provided IT assessment template doesn't encompass every business sector. Specific sectors such as banking, healthcare, telecom, etc., may have unique requirements. These can be addressed either by listing them separately or by incorporating them into one or more existing domains or areas.

Employing IT assessment can act as a crucial initial step and a continuous benchmark, used regularly over time. For instance, conducting an internal assessment annually allows you to review these aspects, adding a column for the current date or the month and year, enabling a clear view of your IT's progression.

As your business and IT landscape grows, additional elements can be seamlessly integrated into the assessment.

1.2 CREATE YOUR STRATEGY

Crafting a strategy is not a one-time effort but an iterative process. By meticulously working on your strategy, you aim to reach from point A (the result of your assessment) to point B in X months/year (s).

I cannot emphasize enough how important it is to ensure that your strategy is clear! It has to be based on very simple principles, like the SMART (stands for Specific, Measurable, Achievable, Relevant, and Time-bound) principle, and has to be transparently agreed upon with your business teams and the CEO.

While Chapter 3 will provide details about how to create your strategy, I want to emphasize its importance and the necessity for it to be clear to you, your team, and the business stakeholders.

Comparing this to travel, we remember that the Strategy is considered Point B, the destination. Imagine you announce plans to travel to "a nice city" by the end of next month, requiring detailed preparation from the team. To you, this "nice city" might be Paris, Rome, or Los Angeles. However, for a team member, it could be their hometown, Tokyo, or Istanbul.

With this in mind, consider the complexities of planning your travel. Each country has its visa regulations, travel costs vary by destination, and the culture and climate of different countries must be considered.

Therefore, if you are not clear about where the team should travel, all efforts—yours and the team's—might be completely in vain. You and your teammates could end up in different locations, each with a different perspective, resulting in frustration and confusion.

Similarly, building a clear strategy is crucial: "Our team should expand by 2 senior engineers and 1 mid-level DBA by the end of Q2". This objective is precise, allowing the team to focus on reaching this specific goal.

Refer to the example of IT Strategy based on Business Strategy provided in **Chapter 3** (Building your Strategy).

> "PRODUCTIVITY IS MEANINGLESS UNLESS YOU KNOW WHAT YOUR GOAL IS."
>
> ELIYAHU M. GOLDRATT AND JEFF COX

1.3 CREATE AND MANAGE YOUR STRATEGY EXECUTION ROADMAP

Once we have a Strategy (remember - it is "point B" where we want to be in a particular timeframe), it is necessary to build an execution plan! This plan should include tasks responsibilities for each domain and sub-domain, follow-up principles, and clear information about what means to achieve the goal. The list of actions to execute the Strategy usually combines into a Roadmap. A well-defined roadmap facilitates breaking down complex tasks into manageable components. For reference, see the example IT Strategy Execution plan - Roadmap in the following chapters (Chapter 4)

A meticulously crafted roadmap aids in decomposing complex tasks into manageable components. For an illustrative guide, refer to the example IT Strategy Execution plan - Roadmap provided in subsequent chapters (Chapter 4).

"IDEAS ARE EASY. EXECUTION IS EVERYTHING." JOHN DOERR

1.4 MANAGE YOUR INTERNAL AND EXTERNAL PROCESSES

Why do I place such emphasis on processes? Many perceive processes as mundane, rule-laden procedures that suffocate innovation and creativity.

However, in my view, a process is far from being a "boring task." It is a mutually agreed-upon sequence of steps, communications, feedback, and tasks designed to achieve something beneficial for the company. Every occurrence in our lives and at our workplace is a process, whether explicitly defined or not. Thus, if we aim to allocate time and resources for innovation and fresh ideas, tasks that are similar in execution should be codified into a documented process. This ensures everyone knows their responsibilities, how to perform tasks, how to address issues, how to offer or process feedback, etc.

While it's unrealistic to expect processes to encompass 100% of work activities, effectively managing 80-90% through well-organized processes can significantly streamline operations and free up time for innovation and new ideas. It's crucial to simplify processes to eliminate unnecessary bureaucracy, making sure employees understand how to meet basic requirements efficiently. Below is an example of a simple process for equipping a new employee with basic tools:

"A new employee in need of a notebook and a pen is directed to a user handbook/FAQ. This resource outlines the necessary information and precise steps for requesting the required items for work and is available from their first day.

Such a streamlined process significantly reduces the time investment required from their supervisor or colleagues. Without such a process, each time the new employee needs something, they would need to inquire about procurement procedures, form submissions, approval processes, etc., from their superiors or peers. It's important to recognize that the absence of established processes can lead to frustration among new hires due to the constant need for clarification."

This example illustrates the critical importance of developing processes. Further details on processes vital for an IT Leader will be explored in the Chapters to follow (Chapter 5 and Chapter 9).

> "THE CIO PARADOX IS A SET OF CONTRADICTIONS THAT LIES AT THE CORE OF IT LEADERSHIP. THE PARADOX ENCAPSULATES THE DAILY CHALLENGES THAT CIOS FACE, AND IT IS WHAT MAKES THE ROLE SO DIFFICULT, AND SO INTERESTING."
>
> MARTHA HELLER

1.5 BUILD YOUR TEAM

Each Manager has a responsibility to properly manage the team which is entrusted to her or him.

Therefore, establishing effective management processes, from hiring to firing, is crucial for team leadership, motivation, and continuous growth. Building and managing the team is an ongoing responsibility—one of the most critical for a successful IT Leader.

Why is your team so important? Over the years, I have heard various directors propose hiring students to build a "cost-efficient" and inexpensive team, believing they will follow orders and thus minimize expenditure, with work being half automated and half manual. Others suggest outsourcing all IT operations to a large company to save time, money, and effort, thereby eliminating the hassle of maintaining an internal IT team.

However, while it may be feasible to hire students or outsource some IT tasks temporarily, relying on these strategies permanently is not sustainable or efficient.

Just as in travel, you need to ensure that your path from Point A (the initial situation) to Point B (your strategy) is sustainable, and that you will reach your destination at the agreed time— not merely by chance! Excuses are unacceptable when we, as leaders, overlook a critical part of our journey: investing in our team. We should reach our destination with our team stronger than before, ready to embark on the next journey with us!

We'll explore the subject of team management more thoroughly in **Chapter 6**.

1.6 MANAGE TECHNOLOGY

In today's business landscape, technology is integral to almost every industry. Properly managing technology is the primary responsibility of an IT Leader. If not managed effectively, technology can become a burden rather than an advantage, causing more issues than benefits for the business.

It's no secret that managing technology is a primary responsibility of an IT or Technology department: selecting, maintaining, and/or building the right Technology for Business.

For instance, if your company requires a solution for HR to manage employee information (HRM - Human Resources Management system), selecting or developing the right system for your business must consider all relevant factors. It's impractical to purchase an expensive system simply because it's deemed the best in its domain without evaluating its suitability for your company. For a business with 20 employees, a system designed for large corporations is likely unsuitable. Perhaps a simple Excel file would suffice to manage all the necessary information.

On the other hand, if your company employs thousands and faces the same HRM needs, proposing a simple Excel file is not viable. Should the HR department require automatic integration with the Accounting system for calculating salaries and bonuses, among other needs, it becomes essential to compile a list of requirements and select a system that meets, at a minimum, the primary needs identified by HR.

Similarly, we must consider all aspects of the business we operate in. Technology leaders and their teams should propose technology solutions that are not only suitable for current business operations but also enable our companies to grow and ensure a sustainable future.

The specifics of managing your technology will be discussed in detail in Chapter 7.

1.7 MANAGE IT BUDGET

The IT budget is an essential tool for organizations to allocate resources effectively, prioritize initiatives, and ensure that the IT department can meet the technological needs of the business. It is usually created in collaboration between IT management and the finance department, aligning IT expenditures with the overall strategic goals and financial constraints of the organization.

The importance of IT Budget planning and execution cannot be overstated - it is something that, if done properly, will enable the IT Leader and IT team to support business growth without restrictions.

Consider our earlier example regarding the selection of the appropriate HRM solution for your company. A company needing to manage information for 20 employees may not require the investment of tens of thousands of dollars in an expensive HRM solution with functionalities designed to meet requirements in various countries. Conversely, managing thousands of employees with overly simplistic solutions that necessitate extensive manual effort is highly inefficient. A portion of the budget should, therefore, be allocated to purchase or develop an HRM system that allows for the proper management of all employee data.

To understand the role of IT budgeting more clearly, let's revisit the analogy of travel preparation. Planning a trip requires us to consider the resources available to reach our destination, as well as our expected arrival time. If our travel budget is $100, choosing a transportation method that fits within this budget is crucial. For instance, taking a taxi might be impractical if the cost is $200. Instead, we might opt for a train or bus, which could cost $50, allowing us to allocate the remaining funds for food and other necessary tasks to reach our destination successfully.

Furthermore, if our journey covers 200 km, opting to travel by bicycle might not be wise; we could arrive much later than anticipated, exhausted, and potentially face risks if adverse weather arises.

To summarize, navigating our journey from Point A to Point B requires meticulous management of the IT budget. Without it, achieving our goals effectively and efficiently would be nearly impossible.

A detailed view of the IT budget and how to manage it will be discussed in Chapter 8.

1.8 IT LEADER ROLES ALIGNMENT

In this chapter, we have explored various aspects of the IT leaders' roles and responsibilities, emphasizing their significance, interconnections with other elements, and the risks associated with neglecting them.

You might wonder **"why these topics are so important for an IT Leader. Am I overlooking anything?"**

To ensure that we're not overlooking any details, we can take a standard IT Leader / CIO Job Description and examine whether all the Key Responsibilities are covered (a practice implemented by Isabel Nyo, CTO and VP of Engineering, when describing the CTO role).

Using this approach, we can review a standard and common Job Description of a CIO and ask ourselves, "What have we covered?" and "Are we missing anything?"

CIO (Head of IT Department) Job Description - Key Responsibilities:

1. **Strategic Planning:** Develop and implement a strategic IT plan that aligns with the organization's overall business strategy. Evaluate emerging technologies and assess their potential to enhance

business efficiency and effectiveness.
2. **Leadership:** Provide leadership and direction to the IT department. Mentor and develop a high-performing IT team to ensure the effective delivery of technology services and solutions.
3. **IT Governance:** Establish and oversee IT policies, procedures, and standards to ensure security, compliance, and efficient operations. Manage IT risks and ensure compliance with relevant laws and regulations.
4. **Budget Management:** Develop and manage the IT budget, ensuring cost-effective resource allocation and cost management.
5. **Project Management:** Oversee key IT projects, ensuring they are delivered on time, within scope, and on budget. Ensure effective change management processes are in place.
6. **Infrastructure Management:** Oversee the development, maintenance, and security of IT infrastructure, including hardware, software, and networks.
7. **Vendor Management:** Manage relationships with technology vendors and service providers, negotiating contracts and ensuring quality service delivery.
8. **Business Continuity:** Ensure robust disaster recovery and business continuity plans are in place and regularly tested.
9. **Innovation:** Foster a culture of innovation within the IT department, encouraging the exploration of new technologies and solutions to drive business growth and efficiency.
10. **Stakeholder Communication:** Act as a liaison between the IT department and other business units. Communicate IT plans, policies,

and technology trends effectively across the organization.

Although the topics discussed in this chapter and throughout the book do not strictly adhere to a ten-responsibilities framework, it is evident that all necessary aspects are addressed. Some chapters tackle multiple elements at once, reflecting their interrelated nature.

1.9 APPLICABLE ACROSS ALL MANAGEMENT STYLES

From our experience, we know that managers can exhibit various leadership styles and employ different methods to manage or lead their teams.

Naturally, you might wonder if a different management style from the author would impact the usefulness of the advice and strategies in this book.

In this book, I choose not to detail various leadership styles, as opinions on their number and nature vary widely.

My leadership style may differ from yours, which is entirely normal. My leadership approaches may adapt to factors such as "season", the company's current state, market conditions, and our objectives. However, responsibilities remain consistent, even though their importance may vary across different "seasons."

The key takeaway is that regardless of your leadership style, the practical advice and steps offered here remain relevant and applicable.

Key Takeaway from Chapter 1: Your Journey as IT Leader

Assessing Current Status: Regularly conduct IT assessments to understand the current state and track IT evolution, and adaptability across various business domains.

Strategy Creation and Execution: Develop and implement a clear, transparent IT strategy aligned with business objectives, including the creation of a detailed execution roadmap.

Process Management: View processes as essential tools to enhance efficiency and foster innovation, illustrated by the simple example of a new employee onboarding process.

Team, Technology, Budget: Direct your focus towards effectively building and managing these critical elements of your IT leadership responsibilities.

Your records: I encourage you to write down your conclusion, ideas, and actions from this Chapter. This action will ensure that the information you get will have practical utilization.

CHAPTER "VS". MY VISION AND VALUES.

In the previous chapter, we examined the topics that will serve as the foundation for your role in IT leadership. Some may be less challenging, while others may present challenges. This variance depends on your prior professional experiences and your strengths or areas where you need improvement.

Before delving into the "puzzle" of the roles and responsibilities of a proficient IT Leader, I'd like to take a moment to encourage you to reflect on two fundamental questions: WHO AM I, and WHY AM I DOING THIS?

Why is this crucial? Drawing from personal experiences and extensive work with various managers and teams, a significant realization emerged - you can execute your tasks competently, yet find no satisfaction in your work, persistently wrestling with tasks or responsibilities. At times, you may question, "Why am I facing continuous challenges despite doing everything right?"

Hence, I urge you to redirect your focus: Who am I, and why are you doing what you do? Consider Your Vision and Your Values!

This isn't about creating something fancy or impressive, nor is it a slideshow to present to management and forget about. I'm emphasizing "your vision" - these two "Vs" should be uniquely yours.

Once you establish this Vision and these Values, they become the driving force that wakes you up in the morning, propelling you to push your capabilities to the limit, to persist in your work even when challenges are relentless.

And these two "Vs" should be aligned, like the well-known saying in the Bible: "A good tree cannot bear bad fruit, and a bad tree cannot bear good fruit." (Matthew 7:18). I've grounded my personal values in the truths found within The Bible.

To craft "My Vision & My Values," you need to pause, stepping away from routine work and thoughts about various issues and challenges. Reflect on what you want to become in 10 or 20 years, what you want to be remembered for, and the legacy you wish to leave behind.

I'm listing some reflection questions that may direct your thoughts to start creating your values and vision:

Q1: What can I do today, the result of which will be visible positively in 10-20 years?

Q2: How can I help my team become the best team we can be?

Q3: As a Leader, what do I do to value my colleagues and their personalities as well as their efforts?

Q4: As an IT & Technology Leader, what do I do to create a significant impact in the company I'm working in?

Q5: As an IT & Technology Leader and citizen, what do I do to create a significant impact in society?

These "Vs" will serve as your foundation, upon which the "walls" listed and described in the following chapters will be built.

To help you build your values and visions, I'll share my "Vision & Values", as an example:

My Vision

- When working with every team, I value each person and contribute to her or his growth, fostering the development of the best team possible.
- In all my endeavors, I facilitate the growth, flourishing, and excellence of those around me.
- I am an integral part of my team, remaining connected through challenges, mistakes, and successes.
- I respect my manager/leader and strive to excel in the offered position and responsibilities.
- In IT, Technology, or Project Management domains (or any other domain), I aim to build optimal solutions, leveraging the team's potential each day, leaving no room for excuses.
- I actively promote the growth of individuals and work to maintain a positive team environment while actively removing toxicity.

My Values:

- I value truth and actively promote it.
- Honesty is a core value that I uphold and encourage.
- I value, provide, and accept support.
- Humility and kindness are esteemed values that I promote.
- Life, family, and health are significant values for me and others.
- Hard work is valued, and I strive to execute tasks professionally without excuses.
- I confront challenges confidently, knowing who I am.

I value these two "Vs" because, in my life and work, they have helped me avoid many troubles, prevented compromises with the truth, and allowed me to stay focused on good values. These Vs helped many of my colleagues in times of challenges and difficulties - when they were questioning if they were useful or not and if what they did had any importance or not.

Hence, I encourage you to reflect on and start the development of your Values and Vision. Even if you choose not to undertake this exercise immediately and continue reading the book, consider revisiting this chapter later and preparing your "Vs."

A time will come when people question the difficulties, challenges, and struggles. Having your "Vs" will empower you to affirm: "We know who we are, and we know what we build, whatever the circumstances are!"

Your records: I encourage you to write down your conclusion, ideas, and actions from this Chapter. This action will ensure that the information you get will have practical utilization.

CHAPTER "C".
CULTURE

In the previous chapter, we discussed crucial elements which define our identity - our Values and Vision. As mentioned before, they are fundamental to us both as leaders and individuals.

To progress on our journey to becoming successful managers and leaders, we need to build upon these foundations.

In this chapter, I want to delve into Culture: both Company Culture and IT Culture.

Since Values and Vision can vary among members of the

management team, it's essential to have cohesive elements that act like glue for the management team and the entire company.

Following Values and Vision, the Culture within the company and your department or team is one of the most critical points.

In other words, Culture embodies the Values and Vision of the company and reflects how we act based on our Values and Vision.

Here is an example of the **Culture of the company**:

Openness and Honesty: In everything we do and say, we are committed to acting with complete openness and honesty.

Transparency: We ensure full transparency in every aspect of our work.

Proactiveness: We don't just wait for things to happen; we take initiative. We act proactively, not waiting for others to make the first move or to speak up. We lead with action and communication.

Trust: Mutual trust is the foundation of our team.

Unity: Despite our diverse roles and responsibilities, we are united as one team. We offer help, provide support through challenges, celebrate our successes, and learn from our failures together.

Simplicity: Simplicity is at the heart of our client services. We handle the complexity of technology and processes internally, ensuring our clients experience ease and clarity.

Based on Company culture, and IT responsibilities, we need to have an IT internal culture sometimes called Manifesto.

It must be at the core of IT teamwork, in every aspect. You may take a lot of examples from the Internet, as many companies are sharing this kind of information.

I would propose one example here, an IT Culture (or Manifesto):
Quality and Excellence: uphold the highest standards of quality and excellence in every aspect of our work.

Adaptability and Resilience: we embrace change, learning from both successes and failures, and we are always ready to adapt to new challenges and opportunities.

Security and Privacy: recognizing the importance of security and privacy, we are uncompromising in our efforts to protect data and uphold the trust placed in us by our users and clients.

Client-Centric Solutions: we place the needs and experiences of our clients at the center of our design and decision-making processes. By understanding and anticipating their needs, we deliver solutions that not only meet but exceed expectations.

Innovation with Purpose: every technological advancement we pursue is aimed at improving efficiency, accessibility, and the quality of life for all.

Ethical Principles in Technology: we develop and implement technology with a keen awareness of its impact on individuals, societies, and the environment, ensuring that our contributions are beneficial and just.

Empowerment through learning: we are dedicated to empowering individuals through education, providing accessible learning resources, and upskilling opportunities to ensure everyone can participate in and benefit from useful technology.

Teamwork, Respect, and Feedback: We recognize that our strength lies in each individual and the collective power of our team. We cultivate an environment of respect and mutual support, where every member is valued and empowered to contribute.

But these are not just words. A technology leader must be the promoter of this culture.

The Culture (or Manifesto) will ensure people know how to be a team, how to support each other, and how to act in many standard and non-standard cases.

Why does Culture or IT Manifesto matter?

For example, simple messages like "They don't understand me" can be changed to "I can support them, I can teach them to understand me or my work."

Instead of "I'm doing my work. They will do their work" we can change to "We are in the team. We are in the same boat. And when I finish my work, I help my teammates".

Doesn't matter. Is it IT or business? I can help them do their work properly with what I can.

Examples of such support:

A lot of times, the things, that matter and help for the team and organization to be efficient, are "in between the tasks" … the tasks which are done by different people.

Meaning that a person finished the work. For example, he/she created an API, and another person should test this API. The person who developed it can construct a bridge (documentation, an example of how to use it).

Now, these tasks are becoming easier because there are a lot of tools that are creating API documentation. And it is easier to do the API, check the documentation, and see if it is right or not. Test yourself, at least once or twice, to see that the API is functioning properly. And, finally, only after you did these steps, transfer the task to the QA engineer, for example.

The same can apply to the person who finishes an important task like "night work" (night planned maintenance). This person, after finishing the work, should write a short information/report:

- there was this change in the platform or the system.
- something (details) was/were implemented.
- new software or update or patch was installed.
- how it was tested.
- what to do if something is not functioning well.
- who is the person who is replacing?
- the rollback procedure is this one (with the description of the procedure)?

In such case people who are maintaining this system and other systems linked to it will have enough information and they'll be ready in case of any impact or issue.

Key point from above elements: Culture in the Company and within IT is important. Now I would like to dig deeper into two important approaches that are often either not done or not done properly: handover and feedback processes. They should be part of a broader Culture!

Culture of Handover.

A culture of handover ensures that every aspect of work within the company is documented, prepared for explanation, and shared with others.

In the domains of technology and IT, security measures like backups are commonplace, where a copy of information is stored elsewhere. This ensures that if the primary information

is lost or erroneously altered, we can recover it from the backup.
Another method of ensuring information security is load balancing, where both the primary and secondary copies of data are distributed across two or many systems. If one system fails, the other takes over the load without any loss of information.

I apply the same principle to managing people's responsibilities within IT teams.

This is referred to as the backup process, as well as the handover process: for all key positions and responsibilities within the IT Department or team, IT leader should organize them as main and backup responsibilities.

For instance, if there are two systems, System A and System B, and two engineers, Alex, and Kent. Alex is more skilled in managing System A, while Kent is more adept at handling System B. Naturally, Alex will look after System A, and Kent will manage System B. This is often where the process ends for many teams...

However, an additional step is required: allocate some time for Alex and Kent to prepare instructions and assist each other in learning how to manage the system for which they are responsible. Once this is accomplished, implement a cross-backup for each other: when Alex is sick or on vacation, Kent will be responsible for supporting System A, and vice versa—when Kent is unavailable for any reason, Alex will take over the support for System B.

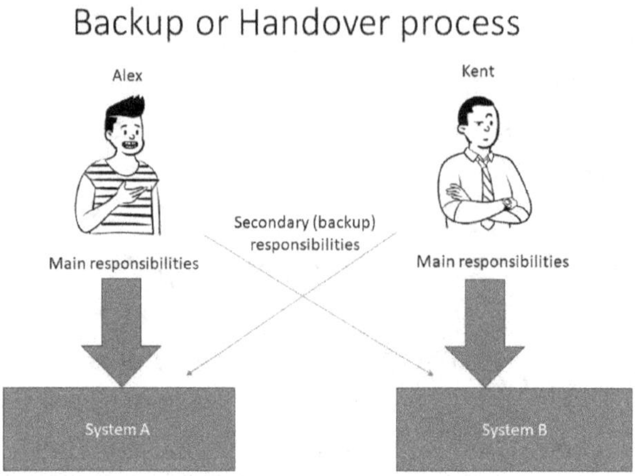

Backup or Handover process

Alex — Main responsibilities → System A
Kent — Main responsibilities → System B
Secondary (backup) responsibilities (cross-links)

Picture 2. Backup and Handover process.

In this approach, you guarantee that:
- There is a reliable backup of responsibilities and knowledge for critical systems and functions, ensuring continuity during vacations or illnesses.
- In the event of a departure, someone is ready to temporarily step in, especially for critical and support cases.
- A smooth handover process is achievable when someone leaves the company.

Typically, the backup person might not completely replace the primary responsible individual but can handle support cases, simple to intermediate configuration tasks, and maintain the system's operational health until the responsible person returns or a replacement is hired.

To make this process effective, it's important for all IT personnel to:
- Document key tasks into instructions and share this knowledge with the team.

- Conduct handover sessions for significant system changes, such as new versions, upgrades, or updates.
- Share critical system information on the Team's shared space.
- Encourage the secondary responsible person to participate in significant system work as part of a shadowing process.

As IT leader, you should promote and oversee this process as a compulsory part of work for every critical area within the company.

Furthermore, it's crucial to apply this approach to your responsibilities. Identify team members who can advance in knowledge and responsibilities and invest in their development: openly share the core aspects of your work, the reasoning behind decisions, budget details, and issues with business and internal teams.

When you're away due to vacation or illness, avoid staying perpetually online (recall your "Vs" from the chapter on "Vs") - delegate your duties to one of these individuals. Rotate the delegation among different team members (based on the size of this group) each time you're away. This strategy ensures that the CEO, business teams, and your teams know: there are people within your team who are capable of taking on new challenges. It also motivates your team members to develop and grow.

Let's Summarize Handover and position backup.

It is important to have a backup person for every key position in a department. This ensures that the work can continue uninterrupted in case of an emergency or absence. It is also important to have a process in place for handing over responsibilities when someone leaves the company. This helps to prevent a crisis and ensures that the company continues to run smoothly.

Culture of Feedback

I'm sure many of you aspire to work with a motivated team—a team eager to excel in efficiency, productivity, collaboration, innovation, and many other aspects that comprise a strong team.

You might wonder, how can I cultivate these characteristics within my team?

A crucial factor is effective communication within the team, primarily through feedback.

As a leader, you must practice and promote feedback.

This can be achieved through scheduled meetings: be it one-on-one sessions, team meetings, cross-team discussions, meetings focused on a specific project, etc.

Yes, I understand, you're already swamped with countless meetings, discussions with business units, and an endless stream of emails and chats awaiting your response.

However, establishing a feedback culture should permeate all meetings, not just those set aside for feedback purposes.

Feedback, in our context, requires:

- Allowing everyone to express their thoughts on any matter.
- Feedback can be either positive or negative.
- Particularly with negative feedback, immediate reactions should be avoided. It might be beneficial to reflect on this feedback for a day, formulate some probing questions, and address these in a subsequent discussion.

To foster an environment where people feel comfortable offering feedback, consider the following approaches:

- Pose questions like "What is your opinion on this?", "What do you think we could do better, avoid altogether, or improve?"
- Inquire about personal performance - "What can I do to make your work more productive and satisfying?"
- During meetings about critical issues, ask "Why did this go

wrong?" and "What can we do to resolve this quicker or prevent it from happening again?"

- When receiving feedback, it's often wise to document it and reflect upon it. Many times, we fail to notice issues within the team simply because we don't adequately consider the feedback given.

- Offer your perspective without initiating an argument: allowing some time between receiving negative feedback and discussing it can help diminish the impulse to argue. Typically, after expressing negative feedback, individuals are more receptive to exploring solutions together.

A culture of feedback is invaluable for bringing the team closer and enhancing efficiency, as it builds trust between team members and their leader.

Let's Summarize about Feedback culture:

Embed a feedback culture in every meeting and interaction. Encourage open, reflective dialogue on all feedback, fostering trust and innovation. This approach is essential for team growth and effectiveness.

To conclude this Chapter, Culture plays a pivotal role in both the operational success of a company and the well-being of its employees. Without a foundation built on strong human values, the consequences can be detrimental. Below you can see examples of Companies and results of having weak or strong Cultures.

Example of a company where the wrong Culture led to a big failure:

One notable example of a company that struggled due to a problematic corporate culture leading to significant issues is

Enron Corporation. Enron, once a giant in the energy sector, collapsed in 2001 due to one of the most infamous accounting fraud scandals in history. The company's culture played a significant role in its downfall. Enron's aggressive pursuit of growth and profits, coupled with a lack of transparency and ethical oversight, fostered an environment where unethical behavior not only thrived but was often rewarded. The emphasis on short-term gains, at the expense of ethical considerations and long-term sustainability, eventually led to fraudulent accounting practices, the concealment of debts, and ultimately, the company's bankruptcy.

This case underscores the critical importance of a healthy corporate culture that prioritizes ethical standards, transparency, and accountability. Enron serves as a cautionary tale of how a toxic culture can lead to the failure of a business, regardless of its size or the industry in which it operates.

Examples of companies that have survived challenging times, thanks to their culture built on strong human values:

Several well-known companies have demonstrated how a strong, positive corporate culture can help them navigate through crises and challenges, emerging stronger or maintaining stability in the face of adversity. Here are two examples:

1. **Southwest Airlines**: Known for its exceptional corporate culture, Southwest Airlines emphasizes employee satisfaction, customer service, and adaptability. This culture has helped it weather numerous challenges in the airline industry, including economic downturns and the competitive pressures of the industry. The company's focus on maintaining a positive work environment and putting employees first has been credited with its ability to sustain profitability and

customer loyalty even during tough times.
2. **Toyota**: After facing significant challenges, including the 2009-2010 vehicle recall crisis due to safety concerns, Toyota's strong culture of continuous improvement (Kaizen) and its philosophy of putting quality first helped it recover and regain its position as a leading global automaker. Toyota's commitment to transparency, accountability, and constant learning played a crucial role in its ability to address the issues and rebuild trust with consumers.

Key Takeaways from Chapter "C". Culture.

Foundation of Values and Vision: Build Company Culture and IT Culture upon the foundational elements of values and vision.

Examples of Company and IT Culture: The importance of technology leaders actively promoting these cultures is evident in the examples of Company Culture and an IT Culture Manifesto.

The Importance of Handover and Feedback: Utilize both handover and feedback as practical elements of IT culture.

Your records: I encourage you to write down your conclusion, ideas, and actions from this Chapter. This action will ensure that the information you get will have practical utilization.

CHAPTER 2. ASSESSMENT OF CURRENT STATUS.

As stated in previous chapters, the IT assessment is mandatory work when you either start your work as an IT Leader, or you start a new season. A new season can be the beginning of the year, changing of business strategy, budget, or strategy preparation, or after some significant changes in the company (a big upgrade, a big launch, a big growth, or failure).
This step should be initiated at the start of your assignment

and can be repeated annually. This approach allows you to track progress, enhance your strategic approach, and address considerations related to efficiency, innovation, sustainability, speed, and security over time.

However, if you didn't initiate this process at the start of your assignment, it's never too late to begin now. Once you engage in this process, as mentioned earlier, you'll be able to monitor your progress over time.

Real-life scenario: The absence of regular IT assessments leads to a crisis.

In a notable case, a Shadow IT system emerged within a company where the primary IT department held responsibility for core systems and oversaw various IT systems and applications across the organization. A specific business department opted to independently develop an in-house sales application, citing convenience and expedited delivery as primary motivations. They argued that internal development eliminated the need for extensive specification iterations and the prolonged wait times associated with IT deliveries.

However, consequences unfolded during a critical sales period when the IT department was urgently invited to a meeting with business directors. The discussion centered on significant problems attributed to the Sales application - numerous clients experienced service disruptions in stores, and sales targets were jeopardized. Understandably, blame was promptly directed at the IT department.

Upon thorough analysis, it became evident that the issues arose from the Sales application, developed internally by the Sales department. This application was not prepared for handling a substantial volume of transactions and lacked optimization for simultaneous use by multiple employees.

In response to the crisis, an immediate request was made for the IT department to rectify the situation by investing in additional equipment, albeit an unforeseen expense.

Eventually, a more strategic decision was taken to transfer the responsibility for the application to the IT department for ongoing support and maintenance. This transition not only facilitated the incorporation of necessary IT mechanisms for capacity management but also mitigated the risk of application failures during periods of high load.

Key takeaways from this story:

This scenario is that a comprehensive IT assessment can reveal functionalities and systems operating outside the scope of the IT department. This realization prompts discussions about implementing essential IT practices for all systems, particularly those integral to customer interaction - usually called Core Systems. By addressing these issues proactively, organizations can enhance their overall operational resilience and minimize risks associated with unmanaged IT systems, fostering a more robust and streamlined business environment.

~~ end of story ~~

How to do the IT assessment

You have to conduct a comprehensive assessment to understand "where we are now" across various domains (see Table 1 below):
- Assess the state of the IT team.
- Evaluate the condition of the IT infrastructure.
- Examine the quality of IT services and adherence to SLAs for both internal and external clients.
- Review the handling of projects and changes as well as operational tasks requested by different departments such as

"company/marketing/sales/etc..."
- Examine IT processes.
- Evaluate the current information security situation within IT.

Table1. IT assessment template (domains listed. some sub-domains listed as examples. You will need to list sub-domains depending on your organization)

#	Domain/area	Priority	Compliance	Action
1	IT organization and staff	1	if the domain is specific, you can list specific compliance requirements	
1.1	IT organization chart. Including number of employees, roles, titles, full or part-time status and local or remote location.		Example: IT structure – done, Team responsibility – done, Job descriptions for each position – done, all employees (internal and temporary included) - done	Example: If something is not done, add actionable item – complete "this" before "that" date
1.2	A description of IT departments/teams with purposes and responsibilities		Example: responsibilities of IT department, of each IT team	
1.3	Capacities, expertise - internal and external		Example: knowledge based on the systems available in the IT environment	
1.4	A list of vendors with proportion of IT expenses		Example: list of all IT vendors ordered by expenses	
2	IT infrastructure and Suppliers	1		
3	List of IT Software (CORE, Additional)	1		
4	Functional and SW architecture	1		
5	ITSM processes			
6	External partners			
7	Information security and Risks			
8	Project implementation processes, Business analysis			
9	Change Management processes, Business analysis			
10	SLA and Incident Management			

11	SW licenses			
12	Offices/affiliates			
13	Call center			
14	Data Warehouse and BI solutions			
15	Warehouse			
16	Testing			
17	Release management			
18	Documentation			
19	Current IT bottlenecks			
20	Current Reports			
21	Future projects driven by Business			
22	Future reports driven by IT			
23	Cost and Budgeting			
24	Software delivery, technical stack (front, back, etc…)			
N	Other domains depending on the functionality in the company (can be payments, data exchange between partners, security requirements, etc….)			

Where:

- **Priority** - set up priority based on your business type. Use 1-2-3 as the priority matrix.

- **Compliance** - documented, process E2E (*end to end*), responsible for each domain, contracts available with clear responsibility matrix, etc. For follow-up purposes Add the Date (MM/YYYY).

- **Action** - based on Compliance - actions to improve, if any. This action should be part of the Change Management or Roadmap process.

Approach this assessment with openness, clarity, and attention to detail.

While this exercise may initially require more time and temporarily divert the team from their routine tasks, its importance should not be underestimated. Thoroughly address each point, as it could prove to be a time-saving investment in the future and help identify potential weaknesses in your IT domain.

> *Note: To conduct the IT assessment, collaboration with all stakeholders within the Business and IT teams is mandatory.*

Working with HR is crucial for analyzing IT staff competencies and knowledge, estimating training needs, hiring needs, or the necessity to outsource some functions to external companies or experts. Outsourcing may be necessary for short-term missions, especially if specific knowledge or experience is urgently required for a project.

It is also essential to collaborate with Customer Service, Sales, Marketing, and Finance to understand their challenges with the technology you oversee, their pain points and success stories, and complete the assessment with the necessary elements and actions.

Simultaneously, you and your team should evaluate each IT domain and sub-domain according to best practices.

Avoid "white zones" - areas that remain incomplete because they are not usually a priority. An example might be a task not initially planned by IT but emerged as a special requirement from the business: managing a company request mailbox where emails directed to different departments need to be forwarded to the respective department heads. If this task, deemed urgent, wasn't automated properly due to time constraints, and was instead handled manually by an engineer, it might become permanent, increasing complex tasks for your IT team.

Such tasks should be reviewed and included in your plan to address all "white zones."

After engaging with all stakeholders and your internal team, the result will be a clear picture of your IT situation—a valuable starting point or re-evaluation marker.

If conducted properly, this assessment can prevent many potential issues for your company and customers.

Key Takeaways from Chapter 2: IT Assessment and its importance.

Evaluate Key IT Domains: Conduct thorough assessments of IT teams, infrastructure, services, projects, processes, and security. Use a template to guide priorities and improvements.

Engage Stakeholders: Work with business and IT stakeholders, including HR, to understand challenges, identify training or outsourcing needs, and gather insights for the assessment.

Eliminate "White Zones": Ensure no area is overlooked by addressing unexpected or burdensome tasks, highlighting the need for automation and efficient planning.

Consider Strategic Outsourcing: Utilize outsourcing for specialized needs or short-term projects to enhance efficiency and focus on core competencies.

Develop an Action Plan: Use the assessment's insights to create a clear action plan, identifying improvement areas to prevent issues and enhance overall performance.

Your records:

I encourage you to write down your conclusion, ideas, and actions from this Chapter. This action will ensure that the information you get will have practical utilization.

CHAPTER 3. BUILDING YOUR STRATEGY

After completing the assessment and gaining a comprehensive understanding, our next focus point should be the IT Strategy - this is "point B" on our map ("point A" is the result of the IT assessment). In this chapter, we will explore the process of developing a sustainable IT Strategy that aligns effectively with your business goals.

Often, we might view strategy as something intricate, complex, or exclusive to the realm of highly experienced managers and leaders, believing it requires vast experience and visionary insight. However, this perception is mistaken. I assure you that creating your strategy and advancing is within your reach.

By the end of this chapter, I hope to instill in you the confidence and knowledge needed to craft a robust strategy for your team or department.

Real-life case: building IT strategy.

A case from my experience: I led the IT team, and they were good, and willing to learn and grow. However, what I observed was that each person was more focused on personal growth. While personal growth is not bad, when it becomes the sole focus, it can become detrimental to the company and the team.

Note: Your team will not be successful if people merely "do their tasks" and then "focus on their personal growth."

Learning from various management pieces of training, I realized that everyone wants to be part of something big, something more significant than just completing day-to-day tasks.

Even when I worked as an IT specialist, I realized... or better say, I expected a strategy for me and my team in line with something big - which is the company's strategy.

Therefore, I've requested from my supervisor what is the Strategy of our company and I've received the company's strategy goals. After meetings and discussions, I tried to understand the meaning of each bullet point of the strategy. Based on the business strategy, I started to build the IT strategy.

Initially, I thought about how to precisely align the business and IT strategies because they are in different languages. I was looking at examples, but didn't find real examples which I could use.

Then I understood that I have to try doing these Strategy points by myself. If I don't try, it will remain unchanged — and that was not an option for me.

Here are some examples of what I did and the logic behind it:

First example:

Business Strategy: Grow sustainable acquisition market share in volume and strongly improve our recently launched offers.

IT Strategy: "Implement and support Roadmap & Innovations: consider internal implementation (instead of supplier), consider cost, consider simplicity for the client!"

Result: IT should prioritize the Roadmap and Innovation, and consider internal implementation, cost, and simplicity for clients in every product it builds.

Takeaways for this example: we built our work around this priority. IT people started working with business teams to understand simplicity, customer expectations, speed of functionality delivery without incurring additional costs, and how to improve product quality through enhanced testing and collaboration within IT teams and with the business.

Another example:

Business Strategy: "Improve the quality of services and differentiate ourselves through innovation."

IT Strategy: (Partially covered in the previous point) + this point is added: "Quality and Capacity: High Availability & Cost Efficiency – maintain preventive protection & implement agreed elements of the 'lean' program."

Result: The IT team focuses on properly managing the capacity of production systems and the quality of all services provided to customers. This involves understanding 'quality for the customer,' not just 'my system is working properly.'

This requires going beyond and talking to the business, understanding their expectations and views on innovation, and helping the business use system functionalities for the company's benefit.

Takeaways from this example: For the team and each individual to grow, they need to see 'where we go.' By building the IT strategy based on the business strategy, we, as IT management, can help people be part of something big, allowing them to grow not just personally but also as part of the team. Their growth significantly improved team cooperation."

As a result of this exercise, we (me and my team) developed an IT strategy that was:

- aligned with the Business Strategy and was shared with the Business departments.

- aligned among different IT teams and known by each person in IT.

- easy to follow - easy to decompose into objectives for each team and each employee, thereby improving delivery, motivation, and engagement of each person in IT, and drastically enhancing cooperation between IT and Business.

~~ end of story ~~

Before we discuss the process of Strategy creation, an Important Note: A strategy may require adjustments or changes during its execution if the business direction, market demand, or regulatory rules shift. Therefore, it's crucial to assess the strategy regularly, which can be done on a monthly, quarterly, or half-yearly basis, depending on the scale of your company/ project.

"PRODUCTIVITY IS MEANINGLESS UNLESS
YOU KNOW WHAT YOUR GOAL IS."

ELIYAHU M. GOLDRATT AND JEFF COX

Here are the recommended steps to follow when you begin to develop your strategy.

3.1 DISCOVER BUSINESS STRATEGY

These are practical steps to get and understand Business strategy.

Consult with the CEO/Founder

Approach your CEO to gain insights into the company's vision and strategy. After doing other steps you may need to repeat this step.

Engage with Business Teams

As you have the information from the CEO or/and Founder, you must work with other Business directors. Interact with your business team(s) to understand: their strategy for the current year (and possibly for several years ahead).

Doing these meetings, please practice patience, actively listen, take notes, and engage in discussions with both business and your teams in order to align expectations.

To engage with business stakeholders effectively, start by creating a stakeholder matrix. Since IT and technology are utilized across all business units, maintaining clear communication, and understanding each unit's usage, knowledge, and expectations of IT and their tools is crucial. For some, technology usage might be as basic as starting a computer and accessing email, while for others, such as in Finance, tools like an ERP system are vital for daily operations, managing financial data, budgets, purchasing records, and more.

Here is a simple example of such a Stakeholder matrix.

DT	Responsible people	IT tools (core, non-core)	Expectations from IT	Information communication
Sales	Director Responsible for Shops Responsible for Business customers	**Core:** Sales tool CRM ERP BI **Non-core:** Invoicing, Email Chat	Tool "Sales" should be available 24/7 Email is used to track clients' requests	Incidents, Maintenance preparation, New projects Or changes linked with the Sales module, Shops infrastructure issues, etc.

Based on your further needs, consider adding details such as communication preferences, escalation paths, and other useful information.

It's essential to maintain a table of this information, not strictly in a document form but possibly within personal records or online notes tools. Having such information simplifies daily IT communications, making it easier to understand needs and facilitating project or change-related interactions.

Dive Deep into Capacity Planning

As the person in charge of technology, the IT Leader must ensure that all systems and applications align with business expectations concerning 'capacity,' which can encompass factors such as customers, documents, traffic, latency, and other key components integral to the technological solution:
- Emphasize the importance of delving deeper into capacity figures, understanding the type and quantity of clients expected

in 1 year and beyond.

- Highlight the significance of IT being as expandable as possible to accommodate business growth.

- Anticipate scenarios where business projections exceed the initially planned capacity, ensuring that your IT infrastructure can scale seamlessly.

Part of IT leadership role is to: ensure you maintain detailed data of all your systems, both production and non-production, including their capacity parameters; record licensing details and hardware capacities—both maximum and recommended; establish a "safety margin" for each parameter, which should vary based on the system, hardware type, or expandability speed.

This information is crucial for budgeting, monitoring, and planning purposes. Additionally, these metrics are vital for your backup and recovery strategy.

This information can be managed using a variety of tools, ranging from basic Excel or Sheets to more advanced ITSM (IT Service Management) or CMDB (Configuration Management Database) solutions such as iTop, Device42, ServiceNow, and others.

In summary, capacity planning is a critical aspect of IT management. For an IT Leader, it's imperative to manage this capacity effectively and communicate its importance to business teams for mutual understanding.

3.2 BUILD IT STRATEGY AND VALIDATE IT.

Once you have gathered the information, meet with your team and possibly your partners to develop the IT strategy:

- Develop an IT strategy based on the information received from the business teams and identify technological elements requiring improvements or transformation.
- Share the draft IT strategy with key team members and department managers, encouraging feedback and making necessary adjustments.
- Ensure the IT strategy becomes a dynamic, working document, not just a presentation for management.
- Remember your "Vs" (from Chapter "Vs") – when formulating your strategy, it's crucial to integrate your values. For a cohesive approach, it's essential to also take into account the long-term vision, alongside the culture of both the company and the IT.

Once the IT strategy is built, present it to the CEO and Business Departments to have full validation:

- Return to the CEO and business departments to present the IT strategy.
- Propose actions aligned with achieving their broader business strategy.

- Incorporate feedback and make required corrections.

As IT evolves, and technology progresses, IT management is no longer solely responsible just for the "technical infrastructure and staff". Technology has become an integral part of business more than ever. In this context, the person managing IT becomes a part of the business.

By following these steps, you will have successfully crafted an IT/Technology Strategy aligned with the business objectives for the designated timeframe, whether it's for the current year or the upcoming one, based on your preparation timeline.

In the Picture below you can see an alignment between Business and IT strategies:

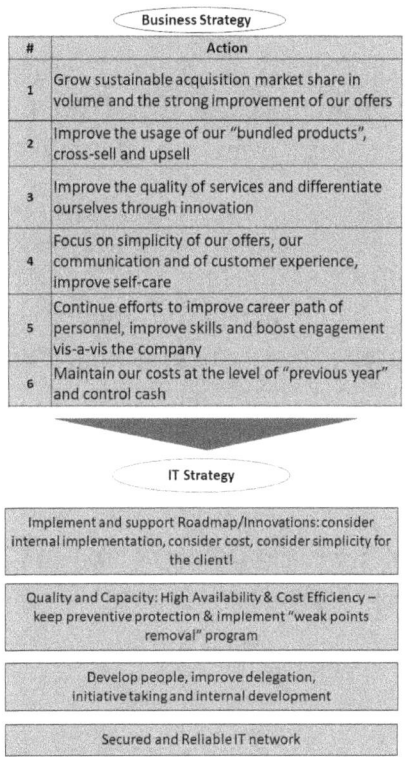

Picture 3. Example of Business and IT strategy on one slide.

Key Takeaways from the Chapter 3: Building IT Strategy

Consultation with Leadership: Initiate strategy development by aligning with the CEO/Founder's vision to ensure IT strategy complements the overall company strategy.

Collaborate with Business Units: Engage with different business teams to understand their strategies and objectives, facilitating a cohesive approach to IT planning.

Focus on Capacity Planning: Assess and plan for IT capacity to support business growth, anticipating future needs and scalability requirements.

Formulate the IT Strategy: Develop a comprehensive IT strategy that addresses insights gathered from business units, includes feedback from key stakeholders, and remains flexible for adjustments.

Presentation and Feedback Integration: Present the developed IT strategy to the CEO and business departments, incorporate their feedback, and refine the strategy to ensure alignment with business goals.

Your records: I encourage you to write down your conclusion, ideas, and actions from this Chapter. This action will ensure that the information you get will have practical utilization.

CHAPTER 4. YOUR STRATEGY EXECUTION ROADMAP

In previous chapters, we've learned how to conduct an IT assessment and how to prepare our IT Strategy, meaning we have identified our current position ("Point A") and our desired outcome ("Point B").

Now, we need to construct a pathway from Point A to Point B.

This involves creating a detailed list of actions that can be monitored or implemented by IT teams and individuals. Maintaining a connection between each action and the overarching strategy is crucial.

Typically, this plan is developed in collaboration with your key personnel and/or managers. You'll review each aspect of the IT Strategy, identifying specific actions, projects, or tasks required to achieve the strategy's expected results.

It's also important to include estimated timelines, the anticipated impact on the business, and which departments will collaborate with or support IT in these efforts.

Remember your "Vs" from Chapter V, considering not only current challenges but long-term Vision & Values too.

To develop a Strategy Execution Roadmap, choose a template that aligns with your and your organization's needs. This can also be done using a Project Management (PM) interface, but it's important to note that this isn't simply a backlog. Instead, each element of the IT Strategy Roadmap should be broken down into one or more actionable tasks. These tasks can then be allocated to yourself, an individual team member, an entire team, or a partner.

For instance, for the IT Strategy objective to 'Implement a new CRM system,' could be divided into several actionable steps:

- Identify critical functionalities of the current CRM system that are essential for business operations. This task could be assigned to the team managing business activities on the CRM, such as Sales, Commercial, Customer Service, or another relevant department.

- Choose a new CRM system. This task should involve the IT Leader and key IT personnel, in collaboration with the Purchasing team and the teams that will use the CRM (as Business owners).

- Implement the new CRM system and transfer data from the old system. Assign this task to a lead technical contact within IT who will oversee the end-to-end implementation, including hardware, system software, database, and network coordination, as well as liaising with business stakeholders.

By following this approach, you can systematically integrate main tasks into the IT Strategy Execution Roadmap.

Here is a sample of the IT Strategy Execution Roadmap.

IT Strategy: Actions plan Hx 20xx (1/2)

#	Action / project	Business impact + comments (if needed)	Timing	Refer to 6 major company priorities	Support/involvement of other departments
1	Keep at maximum the budget figures and ensure savings, if possible		Permanent	6	Finance (follow up, negotiations)
2	Company products implementation. Respect dates of product and solution launch with an objective of (close to) zero default following implementation. Internalize the development as much as possible	Internalization is about 80-90% (several key projects done internally – previously by SUPPLIER)	H2	1, 2, 4	All departments
3	Implementation of Special Project "Bundled product"		H2	1, 2, 4	Marketing

IT Strategy: Actions plan Hx 20xx (2/2)

#	Action / project	Business impact + comments (if needed)	Timing	Refer to 6 major company priorities	Support/involvement of other departments
4	smooth preparation for next Hx 20xx roadmap - mid November – December		November - December 20XX	1, 2, 4	All departments
5	"weak points removal" program implementation	Partially done	H2	3	Technical
6	NEW TOOL pilot implementation	DONE	October-November 20XX	1, 2, 4	Technical

Picture 4. Example IT Strategy Execution Roadmap on 2 slides.

How to Ensure Your IT Strategy Execution Roadmap Remains Current?

As highlighted throughout this book, a strategy is not set in stone; it must align with the business strategy, market conditions, and other critical factors.
Thus, the IT Leaders' responsibility extends beyond merely executing the planned roadmap. It's crucial to ensure that the current roadmap is in complete alignment with the current business strategy.

For instance, consider a scenario where, during a meeting with the CEO and other business stakeholders, you learn about a new regulation requiring shops to issue separate invoices for business customers, including new elements. Such country-level changes often come with strict deadlines. As an IT Leader, you must proactively seek details about who is liaising with regulatory bodies and who is familiar with the requirements and deadlines. Don't wait for business teams to provide all the details spontaneously; ensure they comprehend the complexity and the necessity of understanding these changes in advance to mitigate risks.

This may need several actions within the IT department: checking if your shop software can be adapted to include and print the required information, ensuring the system has the necessary data, confirming you have the appropriate team or partner for implementation, and verifying budget availability.
Regulatory changes should be incorporated into your strategy as they are critical for business compliance. Failure to comply can lead to financial losses or even the loss of the business license.

This example demonstrates proactive engagement upon learning of new requirements.

Another method to ensure the validity of your IT strategy execution roadmap is to regularly organize IT strategy review meetings—known as **IT steering meetings**. These meetings could be quarterly or biannually.

Preparation typically involves a presentation covering, but not limited to, the following points:
- Execution status of the IT strategy roadmap for each item.
- Key performance indicators (KPIs) and reports.
- The current status and main challenges within IT.

Such meetings are vital for ensuring business departments are aligned and they validate the current IT Strategy Roadmap. This guarantees that the roadmap remains aligned with business stakeholders and allows for continued implementation according to agreed plans and timelines.

Now let's see the relationship between the IT Strategy Execution Roadmap and the Company Roadmap

Once you have created your Strategy Execution Roadmap, you need to do the following step: actions that are linked with 1 or more departments should then be part of the Company's Unified Roadmap.

When working on a Company Roadmap, consider the following key elements:

- Design the roadmap with a one-year perspective, detailing actions for the initial 3-6 months. For the latter part of the year, outline planned actions or projects, but remain flexible to adapt based on changes in priorities, budget allocations, or shifts in the business landscape.

- It's crucial to adopt an integrated approach that aligns the Business and IT/Technology roadmaps into a singular, unified company roadmap. This alignment helps avoid conflicts and ensures coordinated strategic planning. An example from Chapter 1 illustrates the significance of this integrated approach. The narrative highlights issues originating from having separate roadmaps, leading to conflicts. The resolution came through the development of a unified, integrated roadmap.

Having separate roadmaps often results in conflicts at various organizational levels, from CxOs to employees, leading to missed targets due to conflicting project priorities.

To address this, ensure a **Single Roadmap** that provides:

1. Unified Project View: Present a consolidated perspective on both Business and IT/Technology projects.

2. Resource Allocation: Clearly outline how resources are allocated across projects.

3. Priority Visibility: Communicate project priorities clearly to all stakeholders.

4. Dependency Awareness: Provide a transparent view of project dependencies.

5. Cultural Alignment: Foster a culture of unity with the message that "we are all in the same boat."

Regularly review the Roadmap and Strategy Execution to maintain control and avoid resource gaps.

Consider the following meeting frequencies:

- **Monthly Basis:** Conduct meetings to discuss and agree on priorities, assess resource availability, and address risks and issues.

- **Weekly Basis (IT/Technology Internal):** Discuss project status, internal and client-related risks, resource dedication, brainstorm new ideas, and outline delivery scenarios.

- **Weekly or Bi-weekly Basis (Business and IT/Technology Key People):** Align teams working on ongoing projects, ensuring a synchronized approach.

For instance, in a project to launch a new service, the Technology team can provide delivery timelines, the Testing team can prepare for testing, the PR team can work on communication strategies, and the sales team can organize training sessions. Decompose the roadmap into individual tasks and incorporate them into Individual Objectives and Key Results (OKRs), with a preference for a 6-month timeframe to ensure tangible results from both Business and Technology perspectives.

Key Takeaways from Chapter 4: Your Strategy Execution Roadmap

Develop an IT Strategy Execution Roadmap that clearly outlines the steps from the current state to the desired future state, ensuring alignment with the Company and IT strategies.

Incorporate IT initiatives into a unified Company Roadmap to ensure coordinated planning across multiple departments, aligning IT efforts with overall business objectives.

Plan with flexibility, focusing on detailed actions for the next 3-6 months while allowing room for adjustments in the roadmap for the latter half of the year.

Adopt a unified roadmap approach to prevent conflicts between business and IT/Technology plans, promoting a culture of collaboration.

Regularly review and adjust the roadmap, employing monthly and weekly meetings to keep the execution aligned with strategic goals and adapt to changes efficiently.

Your records: I encourage you to write down your conclusion, ideas, and actions from this Chapter. This action will ensure that the information you get will have practical utilization.

CHAPTER 5. MANAGE INTERNAL AND EXTERNAL PROCESSES

In previous chapters, we've learned how to identify the current status, how to create your IT strategy (destination) and how to build the roadmap to reach the destination. To reach the destination, plans alone are not enough - you need tools, signs, resources, means to do the work, and people to work with.

What is "**a process**"? As stated in point 1.4 (Chapter 1), it is a series of actions or steps taken to achieve a particular end. In a business or organizational context, a process refers to a set of interconnected activities or tasks that, when performed in sequence, aim to accomplish a specific goal or objective.

This is exactly what we need to build to reach the expected or planned result.

In this chapter, we begin to discuss processes - the means and tools that will help you and your teams realize the roadmap.

As the individual overseeing Technology and Information, the IT Leader plays a pivotal role in orchestrating various processes. While not exhaustive, the following processes are essential.

5.1 SERVICE LEVEL AGREEMENTS

SLAs with Suppliers:

Establish clear agreements compliant with Business and Regulatory requirements for hardware, software, and IT services. Direct collaboration with the Business is crucial to dispel misconceptions about IT capabilities and limitations.

If these requirements do not already exist, they must be developed in collaboration with the business. It is crucial to avoid perceiving IT/Technology as either having 100% availability or being obligated to accept any change request instantly due to Agile practices. The capacity of systems should not be assumed to be unlimited simply because auto-scalability is enabled; there are still limits even in such environments.

As a result, one of the roles of the IT Leader is to guide business colleagues on how to perceive IT/Technology. This involves understanding its functionality, usage parameters, limitations, and the correlation between SLA percentages and capacity/licenses/budget.

External SLA is important!

Whether you are providing services with an SLA, or acquiring services with an SLA, it is a permanent part of any service. Within this wording, there is the term "agreement" which means - we agree to provide OR use the services with this service level.

Real-life story regarding the importance of external SLA.

My team and I were responsible for a platform, serving customers' real-time services.

The SLA for such a platform is 24/7 and it is quite costly. Sometimes, over time, an SLA can cost you more than the platform itself.

But let's come back to the story.

That Saturday, I was called by the Supervision team - "services are down completely." Even though the platform was secured with all necessary (at that time) measures, it was completely down.

A colleague picked me up from home, and we drove to the office and data center.

At this stage of my work, I had all the necessary training, knew how to operate, and could do almost anything with this platform and the OS and the DB inside. But I was not prepared for a crisis - and I started to enter into a panic mode.

Most probably many of you remember this feeling... you open a terminal and think - "what am I going to do right now?" (for me it was the first incident of such scale and with this platform).

Moreover, many people, directors, managers, and teams were waiting for when the problem will be solved. It is Saturday morning, and people are not able to use our services.

At this stage, you understand how important the SLA is!!!

I opened the document, found the phone number and email of the 24/7 support team, and called them.

In the meantime, I collected information from logs thinking: "why the platform is down while OS and DB and Application Software are up and running?" (fast forward - here I was wrong because the issue was with the DB, not running properly).

I called and explained - "we are this and this company, we have this issue". They asked for access - a process that was exactly part of the mentioned SLA. They connected and tried many things which didn't really help.
I was cooperating with them, proposing some actions, and trying together with them, didn't help either.
While trying to solve it, I realized that the pressure is not as intense when you work with the team to find a solution! The panic disappears!

The impact was already about 4 hours - which was a very critical threshold for our company!

My director asked for details and kept me separated from other teams... so that I could be focused on the solution.

(Note) it is very and very important for IT management - when you have an incident, to let your team DO the work focused on the solution, protect them from external questions, and handle the internal communication on your own.

When services are disrupted, the impact on the entire company is substantial.
Retail outlets face operational challenges, as customers, unable to access services, turn to nearby stores for information. These shops, also serving as service centers, are expected to provide updates on incidents and estimated resolution times.
Customer Service was inundated with inquiries, with customers

eager to know when services would be restored. The surge in call volume was so significant that the department had to call in extra staff to manage the overwhelming demand.

From a technical standpoint, if one system fails, others may become overburdened due to a spike in customer activity. Consequently, technical teams must prioritize the maintenance of systems under their purview to ensure continuity and prevent further disruptions.

But let's come back to the incident and see what was next.

The remote support team called their experts, because everything they tried was not solving the issue. Finally, I got on the phone with their database expert, and we started to analyze what was happening with the database… and found out that there was a broken index that didn't react to the command to recover.

It was the first breath of fresh air - apparently, we found the reason!

Now we need to solve it. The database expert explained I needed to get all the services down, put the database in single admin mode, and try one more time to recover this index. This operation could be done only by me because it will restrict all the outside communication.

There were already more than 5 hours of services unavailable.

I executed the recover command… and it worked! The database check passed successfully, and I started to run the services one by one.

The impact was almost 6 hours! Services recovered, and customers started to use the services, which were up and running!

The Takeaway from this story:

Basically, I knew all the actions that were done by the support engineers and their database expert. But in such a crisis, you need a team that can work under pressure, guide you to follow a process, or give them access to do it. You need a team that will confidently, step by step, recover the services.

And for these people and these teams to operate properly, and for services to work properly - you need an Agreement, a Service Level Agreement.

~~ end of story ~~

Next SLA is **the SLAs for Internal Clients.**

An SLA with internal clients can be simple but must be clear. This ensures your team is efficient, and business expectations are well understood. For this, clearly define responsibilities, escalation paths, response times, and communication channels for employees seeking IT/Technology support.

When an employee, have a request that need to be addressed by the IT/Technology team, you should:

1. Clearly understand who is responsible for handling the request.
2. Be aware of the appropriate channels and individuals to contact when making a request.
3. Have a realistic expectation of the time required to fulfill the request.
4. Know the proper escalation path in case the request is unresolved, or the outcome is unsatisfactory.
5. Be informed about the designated application or communication method to use when submitting the request

(which can include email or chat).

Real-life story - Implementation of Internal SLA.

I'd like to share a real-life story about when we implemented an Internal SLA and the outcomes we achieved.

Globally, the company was performing well, acquiring customers, selling, and providing quality services.

The service quality was good to excellent, and all teams were functioning properly.

However ... there were instances when my CEO would call me and inquire why something wasn't working, why customers were dissatisfied, or why there was an incident he was unaware of.

I had to understand the exact issue. After clarification, it became apparent that one of our customers was not activated properly, unable to use our services, leading to their complaints - which translates to 'our services are not working'!

Upon delving deeper, I realized that there were cases where we spoke 'different languages' and perceived services or products differently.

For instance:
- A technical person verifies that systems are working properly, concluding that services are under control.
- The CEO or another businessperson receives a call from a VIP customer complaining about the inability to use our service, interpreting it as a flaw in our services.

We had many cases like this, which didn't improve the working atmosphere. We faced constant pressure and occasional conflicts between teams and departments. Many of you may have experienced this: pressure from management, misalignment between technical and business aspects, miscommunication, etc.

However, with our primary goal being the success of our company and a positive customer experience, we realized the need to come together and:
- Align our understanding of the quality of our service/product.
- Align our understanding of incidents.
- Align our understanding of customer and mass issues.
- Clearly define roles and responsibilities.
- Agree on a process for solving each case with quality, the right tone of voice, and promptly.
- Perform our work with the 'customer in the room'.

Combining all the above, we started building a process called: **Internal SLA and Incidents Management**.

For this purpose, we discussed, agreed, and included in the document (during many meetings):
- Defined all types of issues and KPIs - all aligned between different teams.
- Clarified responsibilities.
- Specified actions for each team when 'this' happens.
- Designated technical/IT responsibilities per domain.
- Outlined how we handle cases: incidents, mass issues (more than X customers), unique customer issues, issues of VIP customers, etc.
- Set timing requirements/necessities for answers or solutions.
- Established an escalation matrix in case the issue/incident is not resolved in time or not resolved properly.
- All done with 'clients in the room'.

As a result:

- We increased our understanding of quality for the client.
- Implemented measures that improved customer experience (such as additional checks after human work and additional tests).
- Enhanced the quality of our products and services.
- Improved internal cooperation - no more ping-pong messages during incidents or issues.

Takeaway from this case:

Even if each team was doing its job properly, we realized that as a company, we were perceived in a fragmented way. Focusing on overall quality and putting the company first in our work through the implementation of this 'Internal SLA' process not only improved the quality and perception of our company but also strengthened our internal cooperation, making us a more cohesive team!

~~ end of story ~~

SLAs for External Clients.

Tailor service quality, availability, responsiveness, and complaint resolution based on regulatory requirements or business needs.

In certain business sectors, these requirements may originate from regulatory bodies within the country where your operations are based.

In the absence of regulatory bodies, such requirements must be established by business teams with the assistance of legal support.

For example, an e-shop website must adhere to the following criteria:

1. Ensure a responsive system, especially during high-traffic periods such as Black Friday or the holiday season, to prevent customer wait times.

2. Maintain real-time synchronization of available stock with purchased items.

3. Provide a 24/7 online payment option.

4. Implement robust security measures to eliminate any risks of compromising personal data.

5. Ensure that all processes, from the moment a customer pays until the goods are received, operate smoothly, accompanied by appropriate notifications, warranties, and so forth.

Technical SLA

Internal technical SLAs apply to all Datacenter elements, encompassing power, conditioning, and other related components.

In some cases, this may involve power duplication or mandatory special conditioning, especially in particularly hot regions. In other cases, another geographically distant datacenter may be required. Only when all elements are aligned with business expectations, IT can guarantee service levels.

5.2 INFORMATION SECURITY

The Information Security process includes, but is not limited to, the following:

- Providing training for newcomers.

- Implementing all necessary security rules based on information categorization.

- Maintaining strict access rules integrated with the hiring and firing.

Upon hiring a new person, an access request should be initiated based on the employee's responsibilities. When an individual leaves the company or takes a long-term leave (e.g., sickness, pregnancy), there should be an immediate suspension or closure of access for that specific person.

How to Start Building an Information Security Program: Begin with Simple Steps.

NOTE: I am not presenting any technical tools here because it all depends on the technologies your company uses. I aim to provide examples of processes, based on my experience and the current trends in various companies I have worked for or learned from.

1. Define Information Categorization and access rules for your company, if not yet defined. This means creating a simple document (later can be detailed) with a table where you list the information you possess and its level of confidentiality for you and your clients. Below, you can see an example of such a table.

Type of Information	Sensitivity Level	Description	Who Has Access (Role)	Who Has Access (Department)
Employee Personal Information	Confidential	Details about employees, including contact information, social security numbers, and personal details.	HR Managers, Department Heads	Human Resources
Client Financial Information	Secret	Financial records and transactions of clients, including account numbers and investment details.	Account Managers, Finance Team	Finance, Account Management
Internal Project Plans	Internal	Plans and documents related to ongoing and upcoming internal projects.	Project Team Members	Relevant Project Departments
Strategic Business Plans	Secret	High-level strategy documents outlining the company's future direction, goals, and initiatives.	C-Level Executives	Executive Management, Strategy
Operational Procedures	Internal	Documents detailing the standard operating procedures, workflows, and guidelines for company operations.	All Employees (as required)	All Departments
Marketing Strategies	Confidential	Plans and analyses related to marketing campaigns, target markets, and product launches.	Marketing Team, Strategic Planners	Marketing, Strategy
Research and Development Data	Secret	Information on new technologies, products in development, research findings, and innovation strategies.	R&D Team, Selected Executives	Research and Development
Financial Reports	Confidential	Reports containing detailed financial performance, forecasts, and budgets.	Finance Team, C-Level Executives	Finance, Executive Management
Legal Documents	Secret	Contracts, agreements, and other legal documents that could affect the company's operations and rights.	Legal Team, C-Level Executives	Legal, Executive Management
IT System Credentials	Secret	Usernames, passwords, and other credentials necessary for accessing company IT systems.	IT Administrators, Security Team	Information Technology

Table 2. Example of Information Categorization.

Where Sensitivity Level is:

- **Secret** is the highest level of sensitivity, used for information whose unauthorized disclosure could cause serious harm to the company or its clients.

- **Confidential** is used for information that, if disclosed without authorization, could cause harm or damage.

- **Internal** is used for information that is not public but is less sensitive than Confidential information; unauthorized disclosure is undesirable but not expected to cause serious harm.

This table serves as a valuable tool for managing information security and ensuring that sensitive data is appropriately protected.

2. Build Basic Information Security Rules for the Company Based on These Concepts: Confidentiality, Integrity, and Availability.

These can be key topics presented to each new employee, among others:

- Passwords for accounts - establish rules for password creation and complexity necessary to prevent guessing.
- Email usage - guidelines on how to handle emails from unknown senders or unexpected emails with attachments, even from known contacts.
- Prohibit running unauthorized software.
- Prohibit sharing access credentials with others.

3. Develop Necessary Information Security Policies (note: this is not an exhaustive list):

- **Password policy** - from day one, implement password rules, especially for management accounts and IT experts, though not exclusively.

  Even though there is a trend towards passwordless access, passwords will continue to be used for many systems for many years to come.

- **Access policy** - based on Information Categorization, construct necessary groups and user accesses that will be strictly required to complete tasks for a specific team, function, or individual.

- **Backup policy** - a policy to back up all necessary data, detailing how to do it, how often, and where to store the backups. Remember to consider regulations like GDPR (General Data Protection Regulation, EU Regulation), which restrict how long certain information can be stored in backups or archives.

- **Encryption policy** - guidelines for securing information within systems, particularly databases.

In this subsection, I've outlined basic steps to ensure your company's Information Security receives adequate attention. Given the current environment, these actions and steps may not suffice, and you may need to collaborate with Security Teams to develop more sophisticated solutions, utilizing SIEM solutions, penetration testing services, bug bounty programs, and others. Discussing these areas in detail is beyond the scope of this book, but you can consult specialized books and articles on Security for more information.

5.3 CHANGE MANAGEMENT PROCESS

The Change Management process must be clear and transparent, providing solutions for various changes. In some cases, the solution may involve addressing the issue in the next sprint or project, while in others, it might entail a decision by the Budget Committee to assess the eligibility of a change that incurs costs, such as system replacement.

This process should encompass IT domains, designate responsible individuals for each domain, establish clear timelines, and include an escalation matrix.

Furthermore, the Change Management process needs to be interconnected with the Roadmap process, serving as one of the entry points (especially when a required change becomes part of a project). Additionally, it should align with internal SLAs, particularly when an issue or incident necessitates a change implementation.

---

real-life case - failure to have a consistent long-term approach to the needed changes.

Throughout my career of more than two decades as an IT Leader, one notable lesson stands out— the significance of laying a solid foundation for processes, particularly when it comes to the Change Management and Roadmap. The impact of a lengthy and unstable Roadmap process on business requirements cannot be overstated.

As the company experienced rapid growth, the demand for numerous applications to keep pace with customer acquisition intensified. However, the Roadmap process in place proved far from ideal. The perpetual shifting of requirements from various business departments to the bottom of the priority list resulted in constant delays in implementation.

Unsurprisingly, the consequences of an unstable Roadmap were felt deeply. Most IT resources found themselves absorbed in marketing projects due to frequently changing priorities. Projects from other departments languished with lower priority, occasionally getting deferred from one year to another.

In response to these challenges, a visionary department head took matters into their own hands. Faced with the impact of lower-priority projects on customer service, they initiated the formation of a dedicated IT team within their department. This team set out to develop applications that streamlined the handling of customer documents and requests across different teams.

Initially, these applications proved highly effective, allowing the department to manage its workload adequately. However, as customer numbers surged, the limitations of the disparate systems became increasingly evident. During peak customer activity periods, processing delays became pronounced, posing a significant risk of losing valuable customers to competitors.

Imagine the following situation: there is a major promotion during the holiday season. Many customers hurry to take advantage of the new offer, willing to queue just to secure a great deal for themselves, their families, or even part of their staff.

They wait in line, complete the paperwork, pay for the service, and... expect the offer to be activated as soon as they leave the store. But - the services are not available. They call after 1 hour - no result, call again in 3 hours - still no result. You can truly understand the frustration when you've done everything required, but the company fails to deliver the promised services.

Meanwhile, inside the company's customer service department, the scene is chaotic: the staff is overwhelmed, extremely busy, and exhausted. Each employee must navigate between 3-4 different interfaces, extracting information from one interface to input into another, then activating something in a third interface, and then... updating information in the first two interfaces again. With such a process, mistakes are inevitable, stress is guaranteed, and delays are a direct consequence of such stressful manual work.

The root of the problem lies in the lack of integration among several systems and applications. Requests flowed through two separate systems, with subsequent processing scattered across various platforms, each requiring manual intervention.

Upon addressing this issue, we launched an integration project. Systems were equipped with APIs to process different request types, ensuring synchronization of all client requests across platforms. The integration not only streamlined the request process but also automated controls and status updates.

Key Takeaways from this story:

1. Integration for Seamless Operations: systems handling client data must be integrated to minimize manual work, enhance control over execution, and bolster security and access to customer data.

2. Early Adoption of Roadmap Process: the roadmap process should be instated in the early stages of the company's growth, allowing for clear prioritization and strategic planning.

3. Prioritization with Long-Term Impact in Mind: when establishing priorities, consider the long-term impact on the company's brand and positioning within the market matrix. Prioritization shouldn't just be about immediate needs but also about sustaining and elevating the company's standing over time.

~~ end of story ~~

5.4 ROADMAP PROCESS AND RELATED ELEMENTS

For the Roadmap process to function properly, several elements must be in place for each company. If they are not in place, the IT Leader should drive this change and propose to implement such processes.

Here are some elements that are key to an efficient Roadmap process:
- **Understanding Project Management Methodologies**: Familiarize teams with project management methodologies to enhance project execution and avoid misunderstandings. Details on the PM methodologies are described in Chapter IX.
- **Components of Roadmap:**
    - **Projects**: Prioritize projects aligned with Strategy Execution.
    - **Events**: Plan for special events requiring preparation and presentation.
    - **Improvements**: Include refactoring, infrastructure changes, and non-client visible modifications.
    - **Changes**: Address change requirements with a clear decision-making process.
- **Programs, Portfolio, Projects:** Align all initiatives within a **Unified roadmap**.
- **Role of Project Management Office (PMO):** PMO should report

to the CEO, and all the departments, including Technology / IT, should align with the type of PMO defined by the company, with necessary internal flows/processes, and established reporting structures.

Here, I want to emphasize an important aspect: the PMO should report directly to the CEO. Why is this so important?

All ideas originating from different departments need to be evaluated, prioritized, and approved at the company level. If the PMO is part of any department (not reporting directly to the CEO) and reports to its director, then the evaluation and prioritization process might not fully consider the benefits for the company as a whole but rather focus on the benefits for that specific department.

When the PMO reports to the CEO, the leader of this team can challenge any department's ideas and present them to the CEO for arbitration. The outcome of such a process will be significantly more beneficial for the company!

---

real-life case of how a Roadmap process was created and managed.

After the launch of the company and its commercial launch on the market, we had several months of "solving the issues," which involved addressing all the problems resulting from a fast and full launch. It took about six months to resolve them all.

Then we created and initiated the Roadmap process to ensure proper delivery of Projects for the benefit of the company.

The process by itself was simple (don't hear "easy" please), but without following the right process, it did not work properly.

There was a dedicated PMO person responsible for collecting all the ideas, project information, and statuses.

PMO reported directly to the CEO of the company - this was

one of the CRUCIAL points. The roadmap was unique for the Company, including projects from all departments!

The Roadmap process was divided into two parts:
- **Preparation of the Roadmap.**
- **Roadmap delivery.**

Below, I'll describe both processes and the result of each process.

Preparing the Roadmap.

Roadmap was divided into Half-Year Roadmap(s) and this is how it was filled with ideas/projects.
- Three months before the start of the next half-year (beg October for H1 next year), each department should provide its list of projects with additional details:
  - Concept of the project
  - Reason for the project - what exactly this project is going to bring to the company/department?
- The IT department also provided a list of technical projects planned for the next period, including migrations, new equipment implementation, upgrades, and new version implementation, among others.
- During the next month, IT needed to analyze all concept documents and provide initial feedback from IT, including complexity (easy, moderate, complex), duration, dependencies, and any key risks.
- After feedback from IT (and other departments) was analyzed and discussed in several meetings, prioritization was introduced, some projects were

removed, and resources were discussed and agreed upon (financial, teams, people, suppliers).
- At the end of November, the Roadmap for H1 was ready and approved, and planning started.
- As projects were validated by the end of November, during December detailed specifications were under preparation - they had to cover at least 3 months of the next Roadmap delivery period.

The same exercise started at the beginning of April for H2.
- With the same sequence of actions, the final approved roadmap for H2 was ready at the end of May.
- (Similar to the explanation above) During June, detailed specifications for the first three months were under preparation and discussion.

As a result of Roadmap preparation:

- All teams knew which projects had to be implemented in the following Roadmap period.
- For each project, there was a confidentiality policy, and responsible people were dedicated from each department.

(Note) The Roadmap covered 80% of the time of people responsible for development and implementation. Why? Because we needed to keep a 20% safety margin for fast projects, reactions to competition, and fast changes linked with some specific events that were unknown in advance.

Roadmap Delivery

Since the Roadmap creation was clear, and we had the Roadmap "file" (you can use any tool here, from Excel / Sheets to Jira or any other) updated and clear for all, it was necessary to organize the Roadmap delivery process properly.

Before going into the details of delivery, several key elements of the Roadmap delivery process:

- It doesn't matter if you deliver projects in a waterfall or agile manner - they all have a start time, launch time, status, risks, allocated resources, and priority. Therefore, the status of the project was important at each stage (details about PM methodology are detailed in Chapter 9).
- Simultaneous projects - it was agreed that there are a maximum of five simultaneous projects in the active phase of development, implementation, and testing at the same It was linked to three elements:
  - Availability of five people inside IT who were responsible for project delivery.
  - Availability of businesspeople to write and rework the specifications and clarify all the details with other departments.
  - Availability of other teams: testing, marketing, etc.

Note - The simultaneous number of projects is a crucial element of the Roadmap delivery process. It should not be too small, as people will be working lightly, and it should not be more than the capacity, as people will not be able to control more details and will not be efficient enough to have a good delivery flow.

- Inside the IT department, there were five people responsible for the project - they were called SPOC (Single Point of Contact). When the project was initiated, one of these people was allocated to the project based on internal discussions we had. This element of SPOC was crucial - this is why: inside each project, there were different IT teams responsible for their subsystems. SPOC was responsible for clarifying, challenging, and proposing solutions for internal IT teams for their project so that the solution would be optimal in terms of cost, and time, and Businesspeople responsible for their projects mainly worked with IT SPOCs. For one project: without SPOC - the project duration could be 7-8 weeks; with SPOC - the project duration was 3-4 weeks.

Now, that key details are known, I'll describe how the Roadmap delivery worked:

Each week there was a Roadmap status meeting.
- The main scope was:
    - Discussion about five simultaneous projects.
    - Removing risks or barriers.
    - Clarifying priorities in case of new elements, ideas, or projects.
    - Reprioritization in case a new project was included in the Roadmap.
    - preparation for coming projects - readiness of specs, experts, and budget.
- People involved:
    - Businesspeople responsible for their budget.
    - CEO of the company.
    - PMO or main PM
    - Main directors or their deputies participate in the delivery.
    - IT Leader
    - IT SPOC people responsible for delivery.
- Before this Company Roadmap status meeting, inside IT, we had our internal Roadmap status meeting:
    - We had to prepare the statuses.
    - We had to prepare the information about risks.

- We had to inform/propose solutions and discuss issues.
- Before the launch of the project, there was a specific meeting, "pre-launch Project X meeting," where all the responsible people had to participate. During this meeting, all the teams were aligned based on a Checklist. In such a way, no delivery was approved if a small but critical detail was missing or not done properly.

Having these two processes, we were ensuring:

- The Roadmap was consistent with the needs of the business.
- The Roadmap was under total control.
- Before the launch, all the projects/products were verified very carefully.

Takeaway from this story:

The process we built was not complex. It was simple and based on agreements between all the departments.

All the statements above helped the company be successful in delivering a very large number of projects. Such a performance was almost impossible for our competitors.

~~ end of story ~~

5.5 TOOLS FOR ROADMAP AND TASK MANAGEMENT

A few words about the tools we can use to manage projects and tasks:

- Utilize tools such as Excel/Sheets, PowerPoint/Docs/Slides, Jira, Trello, Zoho, ClickUp, Confluence (for task management if Jira is used), and Microsoft Project for more extensive projects.
- Don't focus on tools but focus on proper If the process is acceptable, and covers all elements E2E (end to end), then you can use the right tool. The tool itself will not solve a broken process.

My recommendation regarding tools is to choose one that best fits your business and technical environment, offering enough flexibility to accommodate your project management methodology.

Ideally, select the tool that integrates essential elements into a single solution, allowing for (but not limited to):

- Ease of use for the business side to generate new ideas, initiate projects, and monitor progress.
- Simplicity for technical and IT teams to break down tasks, and utilize team and personal boards.
- Visibility and easy searchability of priorities and

descriptions within the tool.
- Straightforward task management, including status changes and the addition of necessary details such as time spent and brief documentation for subsequent processing.
- The ability to create Dashboards, Roadmaps, and management reports detailing project, sprint, and task statuses, as well as reports by user or team.
- A repository for related information, such as BDRs, specifications, and instructions.
- A system for registering incidents and problems and linking them with the backlog.

Most of the well-known tools available today offer these functionalities and much more.

---

real-life case - the implementation of a roadmap/task management tool significantly improved the organization of operational and project work within a team.

While working at a company, I was appointed as the manager of a new team. Though not large, the team's responsibilities spanned various areas: we were tasked with development, project participation, and supporting certain non-production systems.

The diversity of our responsibilities made it challenging to track which tasks were planned, which had been completed, and what remained for any given project or task.

To better coordinate our tasks and manage our resources, we found it necessary to hold separate meetings to discuss statuses, address issues, and plan how to tackle the remaining work.

Although we reached a consensus on our synchronization process, the varied nature of our tasks made us realize the need for a tool to share this information effectively, as emails and chats were insufficient.

At that time, the company lacked a specific tool to meet our needs.

We decided to implement Jira, choosing it for its simplicity and our prior experience with it. I'm not endorsing this tool; there are many similar options available.

We created user accounts for all team members and began organizing our work within the tool.

Setting up was straightforward. We decided on a Kanban board with several sections:
- TODO: All tasks assigned by person and project, including necessary priorities and deadlines.
- IN PROCESS: Tasks currently being executed.
- IN TEST / UNDER REVIEW: Tasks requiring testing or peer review.
- DONE: Completed tasks.

The process was simple:

- Based on priority and criticality, the responsible person would take a task from the TO DO section (backlog), move it to IN PROCESS, and begin work.
- Movement to other sections depended on the task's status.
- The responsible individual was required to document all relevant details within the task: input documents, steps taken, and other task-related information.

As a result:

- We efficiently organized our project and operational work.
- We eliminated the need to inquire about statuses or availability for tasks and meetings.

- We achieved clarity in terms of timing and actions for each task.

This experience highlights the ease and effectiveness of using a straightforward tool to organize tasks and operational processes, significantly improving team workflow.

~~ end of story ~~

5.6 MONITORING AND SUPPORT PROCESSES

Implement robust Incident Management processes, possibly incorporating Problem Management for a comprehensive approach.

Real-Life Story: Enhancing Monitoring and Support Processes

This narrative sheds light on practical steps to enhance the monitoring and support processes within an organization.

Following the implementation of all production systems, monitoring tools began aggregating various issues, including warnings and alarms. While IT experts could easily decipher these alerts, understand and identify the components at risk, the scenario was different for the monitoring and support teams. These teams, tasked with overseeing a broader range of systems beyond IT (such as security systems, specialized applications for retail, customer service, etc.), found each IT-generated alarm to be a novel challenge.

The process for addressing each alarm or warning typically involved contacting a designated IT specialist or even the IT Leader. However, due to the unclear nature of the alarms, misdirected calls were common, leading to frustration among team members who were roused at inconvenient hours for issues outside their responsibilities. This not only affected service and solution delivery times but also reduced team morale.

Furthermore, the situation fostered a blame culture, eroding professional relationships and cooperation, and consequently, service availability suffered.

The root of these misunderstandings stemmed from two main issues:
- Comprehensive understanding of all IT systems and the significance of the alerts.
- The Support and Operations team's lack of detailed knowledge about IT systems, preventing them from interpreting alerts correctly and understanding the specific responsibilities within the IT department.

The resolution involved the IT team developing a process with several key sub-documents:
- An overview of IT systems and services for high-level understanding.
- A detailed description of each IT team's responsibilities.
- An explanation of the different components within IT systems and the rationale for their segregation.
- A guide to understanding alarms and warnings, including the significance of various alerts and appropriate responses.

Additionally, a clear process was established and documented, outlining the steps the Supervision & Monitoring team should follow upon detecting an issue, including internal technical service level agreements (SLAs) for response times.

Following the preparation of these documents, information exchange sessions and on-the-job training were conducted for the Supervision and Maintenance team.

The introduction of these measures led to the following

improvements:

- The Supervision and Monitoring teams became more proficient and took greater responsibility for incident management.
- IT teams were alerted only for critical issues, enhancing efficiency.
- The quality of services improved and became more consistent.
- Team collaboration and cooperation significantly improved.

Key Takeaway from this case:

The importance of a supportive culture and effective communication was underscored. By providing detailed instructions, clarifications, and training, the organization fostered better teamwork and significantly enhanced the quality of its services.

~~ end of story ~~

5.7 DISASTER RECOVERY AND BUSINESS CONTINUITY

In this chapter, I will briefly explore the definitions and key components of two critical processes: Disaster Recovery and Business Continuity.

Although they might not encompass the entirety of your duties, certain aspects of each process should be integral to the activities of an IT Leader.

What is Disaster Recovery?

Disaster Recovery (DR) in the IT domain refers to a set of policies, tools, and procedures that enable the recovery or continuation of vital technology infrastructure and systems following a natural or human-induced disaster.

Disaster recovery focuses specifically on IT or technology systems that support critical business functions, as opposed to business continuity, which involves keeping all essential aspects of a business running despite significant disruptions.

Purpose of Disaster Recovery:

The main goal of disaster recovery is to minimize downtime and data loss to ensure business continuity. By having a robust DR

plan, organizations can:
- Ensure the integrity and availability of critical data and applications.
- Reduce the financial impact of downtime and data loss.
- Maintain customer trust and compliance with legal or regulatory obligations.

In summary, Disaster Recovery is a critical component of overall risk management and business continuity planning, ensuring that IT services can be restored as quickly and smoothly as possible after a disaster.

Key Components of Disaster Recovery:

- **Data Backup:** Regularly copying and archiving computer data so it can be accessed in the event of data deletion or corruption.
- **Recovery Objectives:** Defined by two key metrics:
    - **Recovery Time Objective (RTO):** The targeted duration of time and a service level within which a business process must be restored after a disaster to avoid unacceptable consequences associated with a break in business continuity.
    - **Recovery Point Objective (RPO):** The maximum tolerable period in which data might be lost from an IT service due to a major incident.
- **Disaster Recovery Plan (DRP):** A documented, structured approach with instructions for responding to unplanned incidents, which includes protecting and recovering data, hardware, and applications as well as ensuring that employees can communicate effectively in a crisis.
- **Testing:** Regular testing of the DRP to ensure its effectiveness and to make adjustments based on test outcomes and evolving business requirements.

- **Site Redundancy:** Having physical or cloud-based alternative sites where data and applications can be mirrored or backed up. These sites are typically classified as hot, warm, or cold:

- **Hot Site:** A fully functional data center with hardware and software, personnel, and customer data, capable of resuming operations within a few hours.
- **Warm Site:** A equipped data center that does not have customer data preloaded, but is otherwise ready to receive it and start operations within a few days.
- **Cold Site:** A facility where the necessary infrastructure (space, power, connectivity) exists but hardware, software, and data must be installed afresh.

What is Business Continuity?

Business Continuity (BC) refers to the processes, policies, and procedures that enable an organization to maintain essential functions or quickly resume them in the event of a major disruption, whether due to natural disasters, cyber-attacks, or other significant threats.

Unlike Disaster Recovery (DR), which is primarily focused on the recovery of IT systems and data after a disaster, Business Continuity encompasses a broader scope of planning to ensure the continuation of critical business operations.

Purpose of Business Continuity:

The primary goal of business continuity planning is to protect the organization in the event of an unexpected or potentially disruptive incident by:

- Ensuring the continuity of critical business operations.
- Minimizing financial loss and negative impacts on customers and stakeholders.
- Maintaining brand reputation and customer trust.
- Complying with regulatory requirements and industry standards.

Business Continuity is a holistic approach to organizational resilience, focusing on maintaining operational capabilities under adverse conditions and ensuring the organization can effectively recover from any disruption.

Key Components of Business Continuity:

- **Business Impact Analysis (BIA):** An essential part of BC planning, BIA involves identifying critical business functions and the impact that a disruption could have on them. This analysis helps prioritize resources and recovery strategies.
- **Risk Assessment:** Identifying potential threats and vulnerabilities that could impact the organization's ability to operate. This includes both internal and external risks.
- **Continuity Strategies:** Develop strategies to manage risk and ensure that key operations can continue with minimal downtime. These strategies may involve alternative processes, diversifying supply chains, or arranging for remote work capabilities.
- **Incident Response Plan:** A plan detailing the immediate steps to take in response to a disruption, including establishing a command structure, communication plans, and procedures for minimizing the impact.
- **Recovery Plans:** Detailed instructions for returning to normal operations after the initial response. This includes restoring IT operations, manufacturing processes, or other critical business functions.
- **Training and Testing:** Regular training for employees on their roles in business continuity plans, coupled with testing and drills to ensure plans are effective and that staff are prepared.
- **Maintenance and Review:** Continuous review and updates to the BC plan to reflect changes in the business environment and operational procedures, or after an incident review to improve

future responses.

Difference between Business Continuity and Disaster Recovery:

The conceptual distinction between Business Continuity and Disaster Recovery is presented in the table below.

Aspect	Business Continuity (BC)	Disaster Recovery (DR)
Scope	Encompasses the entire organization, focusing on maintaining or quickly resuming critical business functions.	Primarily focuses on IT systems and data recovery to restore technology infrastructure after a disaster.
Objective	Minimize business operation disruptions and maintain essential functions during and after a disaster.	Quickly recover IT operations and data access to minimize downtime and support business functions.
Focus Areas	Includes human resources, facilities, supply chain, and communication, in addition to IT services.	Concentrates on IT infrastructure, applications, and data backup and restoration processes.

Table 3. Core differences between Business Continuity and Disaster Recovery.

To conclude this subsection, I would like to emphasize that regardless of whether your organization has Disaster Recovery (DR) or Business Continuity (BC) plans in place, an IT Leader should adopt similar practices to guarantee the secure operation of all IT components critical to the company's functionality.

Flexibility and Efficiency should be part of processes:

Regularly adjust processes according to evolving Business and Market conditions. Consider employing the PDCA (Plan-Do-Check-Act) methodology for continuous improvement.

Remember, effective processes evolve with changing landscapes.

Key Takeaways from Chapter 5: Manage Your Internal and External Processes

Service Level Agreements (SLAs)

- **With Suppliers**: Establish clear, compliant agreements for hardware, software, and services. Educate the business on IT capabilities and limitations.

- **For Internal Clients**: Define responsibilities, escalation paths, response times, and communication methods for IT support.

- **For External Clients**: Tailor service quality and responsiveness based on regulatory or business needs, ensuring system responsiveness and security.

- **Technical SLA**: Applies to Datacenter elements like power and conditioning.

Information Security - from day 1 implement the following: information categorization, newcomer training, security rules implementation based on information categorization, various security policies, and strict access control.

Change Management Process - a clear, transparent process that addresses changes, assigns responsibility, establishes timelines, includes an escalation matrix, and integrates with the Roadmap process.

Roadmap Process and Related Elements
Understand and apply project management methodologies, including clear prioritization, planning, managing simultaneous projects, and organizing regular status meetings for roadmap delivery.

Tools for Roadmap Management - tools for managing the

Roadmap are very useful but focus on the process over the tools.

Monitoring and Support Processes - implement robust Incident and Problem Management processes for effective support.

Flexibility and readiness for change – adjustment of processes is crucial to responding to Business and Market changes.

Safeguard continuous and secure operations – consider implementing tools and procedures to safeguard IT ecosystems and ensure continuous business operations.

Your records: I encourage you to write down your conclusion, ideas, and actions from this Chapter. This action will ensure that the information you get will have practical utilization.

CHAPTER 6. BUILD YOUR TEAM

In cultivating a professional and motivated team, IT Leaders should focus on building key values, communication, and key internal processes.

At every step, consider your "Vs" and Culture – long-term Vision & Values, Culture of the Company, and IT Culture - and practice them through these activities.

Real-Life Story - Building your team with simple Cultural values.

I'm sharing a story from the early days of my management career. I was part of the IT division in a company that faced numerous challenges, including financial issues, organizational problems, and a risky position in the market.

A new CEO was appointed, and all members of the company's management team were convened for a meeting to acquaint ourselves with the new company leader.

Typically, a new leader spends around three months (90-100 days) to grasp the company's situation (akin to an IT assessment process, but broader) before taking significant leadership steps. During these initial months, we operated as usual: different departments and teams conflicted, and projects were slow to start, and even slower to implement due to these disputes. Each team or department viewed their work as paramount, often undermining the significance of others whenever possible.

Surprisingly, we considered such dynamics "normal". We recognized our contributions as significant but viewed the efforts of others as less so. Consequently, it was challenging to consider, adapt, or implement the ideas of others.

As mentioned, the CEO spent around three months assessing the situation. Then, at the beginning of the year—a time when we typically reviewed the previous year's results and discussed strategies or visions for the coming year—we had a common meeting.

However, this meeting deviated from the norm.

The meeting started in a familiar manner, but the latter half was entirely different. The new boss outlined his perception of the current situation, echoing my earlier description: conflicts, lack of commitment, absence of communication, no teamwork, reactive approaches, insufficient planning, a culture of blame, "ping-pong" behaviors, and indirect work, with employees constantly complaining to their direct managers.

This situation was clearly harmful to both the company and its teams.

He then introduced new company rules—a **new culture** upon which we would base our work:
- **Teamwork**: Achieve results together.
- **Proactiveness**: Move beyond reactive work.
- **Horizontal Collaboration**: People should work directly with their peers from other departments, bypassing the need for supervisory mediation.
- **No Blame Game or Complaining**: Address issues directly and attempt to resolve them. Escalate only if direct resolution fails.

He requested each manager to adhere to these rules and to disseminate the new culture throughout the company, encouraging everyone to adopt these new approaches.

Naturally, we were somewhat skeptical about the new rules, doubting that much would change. Nevertheless, we complied and began to integrate the new culture into our daily work.

Fast forward one year later: our market position had not only improved, but we had also become the leader, unreachable by our competitors.

The company had transformed into a complete and unified team!

What actually changed:

- The rules against complaining and "ping-pong" emails led us to address complex questions in meetings instead of lengthy email threads, significantly reducing our email backlog and resolving many issues.
- Proactiveness encouraged us to think ahead about improvements, new projects, or ways to support business departments in resolving issues.

- Horizontal collaboration allowed us to work with peers from other departments without constantly seeking managerial approval. This isn't to say actions shouldn't be communicated to managers, but rather, the work itself—responding to an email, organizing a meeting on a new project, explaining feasibility—didn't always require a manager's direct involvement.

The Takeaway from this case:

Often, we fear simplicity, but sometimes, simple principles need to guide our day-to-day work. Embracing a culture where we view ourselves as a team, value each other, and focus on solving issues rather than complaining, can empower a team to exceed expectations and achieve remarkable success.

~~ end of story ~~

To build the team you need Values and Culture, as well as tailored and clear processes.

Here are some essential practices to consider.

6.1 HIRING PROCESS

Hiring can be a "scary" process, as it involves bringing in new people, ensuring that the candidate meets your requirements, and hoping that the person will remain with the company and perform their duties effectively. Therefore, it's crucial to approach the hiring process carefully.

Here are some suggestions on how to achieve truly positive outcomes:

- Review candidates' CVs: Resumes/CVs should be reviewed by the IT Leader or a designated responsible individual to ensure a thorough assessment.
- Bypassing HR Hurdles: While involving HR in the hiring process, the technology-centric aspects should be overseen by those with a technical background to prevent misunderstandings.
- Efficient and Transparent Processes: Streamline the hiring process for professionals by making it transparent, efficient, and aligned with the team's needs.

Key point: as much as possible, try to reduce the timing between the interview and work offer, especially for key positions.

Real-life example of my hiring practice.

Hiring can be a significant challenge for many companies, particularly when it comes to recruiting IT professionals with both experience and a willingness to change jobs. While

HR teams are typically tasked with handling this process, based on my experience, relying solely on HR in the hiring process is a mistake.

In my managerial roles, I observed the struggles of other departments and IT management in securing the right professionals. Sometimes, the process took over a year to fill a position.

Here is how I approached this challenge:

- I collaborated with HR to ensure they played their part in preparing the Job Description, posting announcements, and undertaking recruitment tasks, such as searching social networks and liaising with other recruiters.
- All CVs received for a position were meticulously reviewed by either myself or a designated colleague from my team. We verified the candidates' experience, technical expertise, and suitability for the position. It was the first step!
- Following the CV review done by IT, potential candidates were selected, and HR then organized interviews.

The interview process involved an initial meeting with HR (which is mandatory as an introduction for the new candidate), followed by a technical interview with either the technical team or me, depending on availability. These interviews were conducted on the same day. Technical interviews included both testing and general questions about experience and knowledge. During the testing period, no mobile phones or notebooks were allowed.

- For selected candidates, a security check was conducted by the designated Security responsible.
- Once the security check was completed, a tailored job offer was extended to the candidate.

About the interview process:

- Throughout the interview process, we emphasized a professional attitude and kindness with each candidate.
- Punctuality was crucial, and it was essential to avoid adopting an authoritative attitude; instead, a polite demeanor was maintained.
- Providing comprehensive details about the company during the interview was considered crucial. Important information should not be withheld, as discovering vital details after joining can lead to dissatisfaction among employees.

About the salary negotiation, I took the following approach: if the candidate's requested salary is below the figure planned by the company, it was a practice to offer a higher salary. Many candidates may hesitate to ask for a higher salary initially, but providing a competitive salary upfront contributes to improved motivation.

Takeaways from this approach:

This approach to the interview and the candidate has proven effective, resulting in the successful hiring of numerous individuals who contributed significantly to the company's growth, benefiting both the organization and the individuals themselves.

~~ end of story ~~

6.2 MANAGE CONTINUOUS LEARNING - HARD AND SOFT SKILLS

Everything is evolving! You and your team need to possess the knowledge and skills to tackle the real challenges of today and tomorrow, rather than relying solely on what was learned yesterday. Therefore, fostering a culture of continuous learning is crucial both for the company as a whole and for every team member.

Consider the following two points to address this topic:

- **Training Plans:** Develop and sustain a comprehensive training plan based on team knowledge, business and technology trends, and essential soft skills to enhance teamwork, focus, and motivation.

- **Lead by Example:** Active participation in training fosters a culture of continuous Team members following their leader's commitment to learning.

As a leader, you can engage in training, particularly when it involves new technologies or the next generation of technology. However, this alone is not sufficient. You should also undertake additional activities, focusing internally on what's new in your field, what others are doing, the latest technology trends, and the improvement methodologies or technologies that have helped other companies become more efficient and effective.

Furthermore, maintain openness with your team members. When they suggest something new, engage by asking questions and seeking advice on why this might be better than other options or the current approach, and why they believe it's interesting or important to adopt. Through such discussions, you may gain a wealth of new insights and encourage your teams to share information freely and be prepared to assume responsibility.

6.3 IMPLEMENT SALARY STRUCTURE AND CAREER PATH.

Salaries for technology employees are a key point of motivation and a reflection of their value.

Therefore, consider these two aspects:

- **Market-Aligned Salaries:** Ensure that salaries align with market standards and the cost of living in the specific geographic location.

- **Balanced Compensation:** Design a system with components such as salary, performance evaluation, and bonuses, with clear visibility into potential career paths.

Salary grid **example**

Employee grade	Minimum knowledge	Salary range	Level up condition
Q&A Engineering team			
Junior 1	• Basic Knowledge of QA • Analytical thinking • Basic knowledge about Information Technology from both software and hardware perspective • Understanding of required tasks • Ability to learn fast	250–350	• During evaluation • Result of project
......			
Middle 1		00-900	
......			
Senior 1,2,3, TL		1500-2500	
Development team			
Junior 1		300-400	
......			

Salary modification – once a year as rule (with possible exceptions). For Junior positions can be set - twice a year.

Table 4. Salary Grid Example.

6.4 IMPLEMENT MOTIVATIONAL SYSTEMS

You and your team will encounter various situations, crises, issues, and successes. One element that will help you maintain the proper work attitude is your motivational strategy for each individual - a motivational system!

Consider implementing several of the approaches presented below.

- **Transparent Salary Grid:** Develop a visible salary grid based on position and level for each employee level, providing clarity on achievement expectations and potential salary increases.

- **Performance Evaluation System:** Establish a transparent system tied to the roadmap and strategy execution, with clear objectives and a link to the bonus system.

- **Bonus System Logic:** Align bonuses with positions, attributing higher percentages to higher positions to recognize their greater impact on company results.

- **Tailored Talent Management:** Create a specific talent management matrix for key team members, addressing individual motivational factors.

Real-life Case About This Motivational System.

Motivation stands as a pivotal topic for every manager.

Over years of experience, I've come to realize that motivation should not be short-term, such motivation inevitably fades away. It is essential to construct a long-term motivational engine or system.

While there are various motivational methods, my preference leans towards simplicity and clarity: basing motivation on an individual's identity, actions, and aspirations.

Hence, in most of the companies I've worked for, with each team and individual, I established a program grounded in:
- Salary
- Performance Evaluation
- Bonus

Let's delve into each topic separately:

Salary - While everyone appreciates a good salary, its motivating impact diminishes over time, often perceived as a routine payment for one's work.

Therefore, instead of a simple salary, we transform it into a Salary Grid & Career Path (an example of a Salary Grid is Table 4.).

Formally executed by HR for the entire company, I utilized it as a vital component of the motivational system. The message conveyed was that this is a potential career path, providing each person with visibility on how they can progress in terms of position, knowledge, and salary increase.

(Note) Try to leverage existing elements within your company! Not every new idea necessitates new implementation or new components. A change in perspective, without manipulation, can significantly alter people's outlook.

Performance Evaluation - another tool typically managed by HR within each department.

This could become a futile task, consuming time without yielding meaningful results, if not executed properly, if not considered thoughtfully, or if the focus is solely on the bonus component rather than the individual.

I use Performance Evaluation as a tool to:
- Communicate with each individual about personal growth.
- Communicate about company strategy, emphasizing being part of something significant.
- Communicate about the success of the company, team, and individual.
- Engage in open and direct discussions about areas for improvement.

Even without a substantial bonus attached to this process, individuals understand that they are valued, their work is appreciated, their concerns are acknowledged, and efforts to facilitate their growth are supported.

The final segment of this motivational system is the bonus part.

Certainly, when it comes to monetary rewards, having an approved budget is crucial. Not every time was it sizable enough to meet my desire to recognize the team, but here's the key - honesty and genuine care make even a small bonus highly valuable.

As a Result:

People were eager to grow, with the growth path visible to each of them. They worked as a team, translating into more success for the team, the company, and for each individual. Their willingness to introduce new ideas and adopt fresh approaches was a testament to the growth they experienced.

Takeaway from this story: Motivation should be grounded in a long-term approach. Cultivating a culture of care, utilizing standard elements of our work with a caring approach, allows the construction of a robust motivational tool. There's no need to create something new each time; a consistent and thoughtful approach motivates individuals to work and grow.

~~ end of story ~~

I need to highlight something about the bonus program.
The example I provided might not be applicable across all companies or industries.

You could adopt various methodologies, such as:
- Conducting performance evaluations for employees and assigning bonuses quarterly - to enhance motivation and focus, whereas for managers, performance evaluations and bonuses could be annual to encourage long-term actions and a focus on company results.
- Planning bonuses for the successful implementation of significant projects.
- Allocating bonuses for achieving strong results at the year's end.

Regardless of the performance evaluation and bonus system you develop, ensure it is relevant to your team's work and motivates each individual to contribute as part of the team.

6.5 MANAGE PROPERLY COMMUNICATION AND MEETINGS

Effective communication is essential in every aspect of your work.

When properly managed, it ensures that irrespective of the circumstances, teamwork and performance remain unaffected.

- **Open Communication:** Maintain open and regular communication with teams and individual team members.
- **Mandatory Meetings:**
  - **Regular 1-to-1 performance evaluation meetings**, emphasizing constructive feedback – at least 2 times a year.
  - **Department-wide meetings** to set the stage for performance evaluations, discuss company strategy, and outline departmental priorities - at least 2 times a year.
  - **Weekly meetings with direct reports** to share updates and ensure everyone has a voice.
  - **Weekly project meetings** with key team members to evaluate the status of projects and discuss new ideas.

- **Regular meetings with other department managers or directors** for cross-functional communication – the frequency can be monthly unless a more frequent cadence is deemed necessary.
- **Ad-hoc Meetings:** Conduct meetings as needed, such as project evaluations, crises, celebrations, and 1-to-1 sessions with individuals who require support or have underperformed.

Remember, the success of your team relies on adaptable and responsive leadership. Keep processes dynamic, aligning them with changing business and market dynamics.

6.6 RETENTION STRATEGIES

In this chapter, we've explored various aspects related to managing your team. A critical issue we must address is - how to retain team members, particularly key personnel and talented individuals.

Real-Life Example of Successful Retention Strategy and Actions

This example highlights an individual who chose to remain with the company for many years, despite being highly qualified and receiving attractive offers elsewhere.

Initially, the interview process was conducted with openness and transparency, including necessary tests and clear communication. The job description, company culture, rules, and benefits were thoroughly explained during the interview.

Upon accepting the offer, the transition into the company was seamless, with no surprises.

Given our responsibility for several complex systems in IT, comprehensive professional training was provided, allowing this individual and other new hires to focus solely on acquiring knowledge and achieving the best possible results without distractions.

In the following months, this individual not only excelled in his training results but also demonstrated a professional and positive attitude towards the systems, operations, team, and company policies. His ability to work well within the team quickly elevated him to a leadership position, thanks to his dedication and professionalism.

When HR and I developed the talent and career development chart for key personnel, this individual was among those selected. For each listed person, we assessed their career aspirations and needs from the personal and company's perspective, focusing on:

- Compensation & Benefits: salary, car, loans, and other perks.
- Career Development: promotions, positional or grade changes, opportunities for mobility within the organization.
- Professional Development: targeted pieces of training for new skills and knowledge acquisition.
- Recognition: awards for outstanding performance, new roles, etc.
- Work/Life Balance: ensuring a healthy balance between work responsibilities and personal life.

Every six months, we planned actions targeting one or two of these elements. For instance, selecting points 1 and 3 might involve offering a loan option or compensation for personal learning initiatives and recommending 2-3 specific professional training programs tailored to the individual.

These proposals were typically made during the evaluation phases.

Subsequently, HR and I reviewed the outcomes every six months, focused on talents and key personnel, and prepared action plans for the upcoming period.

Note: Most management and leadership efforts may go unnoticed by the team, but the outcome of this work is a strong, high-achieving team!

Over the next three years, HR and I periodically undertook such initiatives. The individual not only progressed and remained with our company but also delivered outstanding work, becoming a key asset not just to the IT department but to the entire company. It's worth noting that during this period, the person received several competitive offers but chose to stay because of the company's continued investment and effective retention strategies implemented over the years.

Here is an example of a successful retention strategy and its outcomes.

~~end of the story~~

We discussed several retention strategies earlier: effective hiring practices, a competitive salary and compensation (bonuses and social package) a clear salary grid to outline career progression performance evaluation, and bonus programs to boost engagement, along with proper communication and a talent management program. These methods are crucial for implementation in one form or another.

However, even with these measures, we're not fully protected from staff turnover, which is notably high among IT experts today.

To develop and refine a strategy for mitigating staff turnover, a comprehensive approach is necessary. This strategy should aim to understand turnover's root causes, introduce specific retention measures, and continually adapt these strategies based on feedback and results.

To further enhance retention, we should (assuming we have already implemented the elements discussed previously):

Identify the Causes of Turnover:
- **Employee Feedback Mechanisms:** Leverage

surveys, suggestion boxes, and regular check-ins to collect ongoing employee feedback.
- **Exit Interview Analysis**: Systematically gather and assess exit interview data to pinpoint prevalent departure reasons.
- **Turnover Trend Analysis**: Review turnover statistics to spot patterns or departments with elevated turnover rates for focused interventions.

Enhance Onboarding:
- **Structured Onboarding Experience**: Create a welcoming onboarding process that integrates new hires with the company culture and their peers from the outset.

Promote Career Development and Growth:
- **Individual Growth Plans**: Work with employees to tailor personalized career advancement plans.
- **Professional Development Opportunities**: Provide access to training, workshops, and continuing education.
- **Mentorship and Coaching**: Initiate mentorship programs pairing employees with seasoned mentors for advice and support.

Boost Employee Engagement and Satisfaction:
- **Regular Engagement Surveys**: Periodically conduct surveys to gauge engagement levels and pinpoint improvement areas.
- **Team-Building Activities**: Organize events that foster team unity and a sense of belonging.
- **Empowerment Practices**: Engage employees in decision-making and grant them autonomy over their tasks.

Combat Burnout:

- **Proactive Workload Management**: Actively monitor and manage workloads to prevent employee overload.
- **Managerial Support**: Equip managers to identify burnout signs and offer necessary support to their teams.

Implementing this detailed strategy can help tackle the complex issue of staff turnover in the IT sector, creating an environment that nurtures retention, engagement, and long-term dedication.

Key Takeaways from Chapter 6: Build Your Team

Hiring Process Enhancements: Refine the hiring process to make it transparent and efficient, ensuring the right fit for the team while reducing the time from interview to job offer.

Promoting Continuous Learning: Keep the focus on continuous learning through developing comprehensive training plans and leading by example.

Salary Structure and Career Paths: Align salaries with market standards and provide clear visibility of career progression paths to motivate and retain talent.

Implementing Motivational Systems: Beyond salary, enhance motivation with a performance evaluation system aligned with company strategy, impact-based rewards, and personalized talent management to meet individual motivational needs.

Effective Communication and Meeting Management: Ensure effective communication through open dialogue, and regular individual, and team meetings.

Implement efficient retention strategies: Maintain a focus on staff retention by adopting essential practices to keep your team members.

Your records: I encourage you to write down your conclusion, ideas, and actions from this Chapter. This action will ensure that the information you get will have practical utilization.

CHAPTER 7. MANAGE TECHNOLOGY

While this guide won't delve into intricate analyses of software, data center versus cloud options, or the selection of specific databases, its focus is on providing practical insights for proper technology management.
Here are key considerations.

7.1 MANAGE THE BORDERS OF IT

As an IT Leader, you are responsible for managing the company's technology.

Typically, there are two areas of technology management:

- **Internal**: This refers to the technology used within the company, such as IT equipment, software, licenses, etc.

- **External**: This pertains to technology provided by partners, including the technology solutions your company receives, alongside contracts and Service Level Agreements (SLAs).

Before delving into details for each area, I will share a real-life experience of managing the external aspect.

Real-life case - a crucial collaboration between IT and Purchasing from day one.

On this subject, I'm sharing insights from a remarkable venture I undertook at the company – launching a new Telecom Operator in an entirely new country, a complete Greenfield Start-up. This endeavor presented a unique market with its complexity, advantages, and challenges, offering IT professionals an ideal platform to create from scratch, ensuring everything from equipment to technology and processes aligned seamlessly.

Within this dynamic environment, one of my key responsibilities as CIO was to purchase IT equipment, covering user devices (PCs, notebooks, monitors, etc.) to Datacenter IT equipment (network gear, servers, storage, etc.). I want to underscore the critical role played by the Purchasing team in such challenging scenarios. Even for adept IT professionals equipped with a comprehensive understanding of needs, architectural expertise, and a readiness to organize purchases, collaboration with a Purchasing team is necessary due to various considerations:

- **Building Strong Business Relationships:**

Partnering with a vendor requires establishing lasting business relationships to ensure responsibilities are fulfilled effectively.

- **Beyond the Price War:**

The allure of low prices during a "price war" can be misleading. Long-term considerations such as support, parts replacements, and warranty expenses necessitate a thorough evaluation of the Total Cost of Ownership (TCO) over 3 or 5 years.

- **Navigating Tricky Suppliers:**

In a new market, dealing with unknown suppliers necessitates caution. Purchasing teams act as a safeguard, enforcing compliance with requirements and preventing potential pitfalls like special tricks or shortcuts.

Our approach involved initiating an RFP (Request for Proposal), where Purchasing took charge of the process. This involved crafting RFP specifications based on technical and business requirements, sending them to potential service providers, and evaluating proposals based on predetermined conditions and timelines.

During the relatively brief RFP duration, spanning

approximately a month due to the urgency of the situation, our focus encompassed the following key actions:
- Conducting meetings with potential suppliers.
- Analyzing the offers and accompanying documentation.
- Scrutinizing their actual capabilities vis-à-vis their proposals.

At first glance, all seemed to be more or less professional, capable of fulfilling our requests.

However, through our collaboration with the Purchasing team, we unearthed critical insights:

- **Identification of "Fake Companies":** uncovering several entities operating as part of a larger conglomerate engaged in deceptive competition and pricing tactics. Prohibited by RFP rules, these companies were coordinating proposals within their group, leading to disqualification. This underscored our commitment to finding a partner rather than merely opting for the cheapest prices.

- **Warranty and Support Deception:** unearthing a company falsely claiming compliance with our warranty and support requirements, despite having a small support team of only four engineers presented a substantial risk, particularly for services that rely on local engineers.

- **Reluctance to Maintain Spare Parts Stock:** identifying companies unwilling to uphold a stock of spare parts, a crucial This not only aligned with our needs but also was easily organized by sourcing from larger suppliers like HP or DELL, who willingly included spare parts in larger quantities.

The challenge extended beyond meeting requirements; it delved into the willingness of potential partners to share risks. We emphasized our quest for a partner genuinely prepared to collaborate on risk-sharing.

Following numerous meetings and calls, we eventually narrowed down our choices to two players with compelling offers and favorable Total Cost of Ownership (TCO) considerations—a pivotal factor in our purchasing strategy, emphasizing the importance of evaluating costs over time.

Selecting a supplier, accepting their offer, and initiating the delivery process became the next critical steps.

The date on the calendar was December 25th. In the country where we were working, it was not a holiday. However, one of the two pre-selected suppliers explained that they would not work on the purchase offer because their partners in the EU were on holiday. As a result, they stated that they would commence work after January 3rd of the following year.

The decision was made easier when another supplier demonstrated a readiness to commence work, even during this holiday period - an indication of a partner willing to make sacrifices, understand our needs, and potentially evolve into a valuable long-term collaborator for our company.

As a result, we have found a partner who not only delivered all the necessary items on time but has also proven to be one of the best partners in the country over the years!

Key Insights and Takeaways from this case:

Collaboration Between IT and Purchasing: successful outcomes require seamless collaboration between IT and Purchasing to ensure all conditions are met.

Specialized Tools and Knowledge: purchasing teams possess unique tools and knowledge crucial for thoroughly assessing potential partners beyond their ability to deliver equipment.

TCO Over Initial Cost: evaluating offers should extend beyond the immediate price benefits. Understanding of TCO over 3 or 5 years provides a comprehensive view for decision-making.

Choosing a Partner, Not Just a Supplier: recognizing the value of a long-term partnership over a mere "equipment delivery" arrangement is paramount for sustained success.

This experience underscores the significance of a robust partnership between IT and Purchasing, leveraging their respective strengths for informed decision-making and long-term success.

~~ end of story ~~

Now let's delve into the details of both domains: Internal and External.

- Internal:

Establish clear policies with the CEO and CxOs regarding "Who is responsible for Company Technology purchasing/management/selection?" to prevent conflicts, cost increases, and incidents.

Ensure collaboration with non-Technology leaders, especially in the context of cloud solutions, avoiding siloed decision-making and potential integration challenges. Agree that the IT department is responsible for setting requirements, participating in selection processes, and maintaining all software and IT hardware solutions.

- External:

- Identify trusted partners to share responsibility for specific aspects, like warranty and support of equipment or solutions.

Select suppliers for PC/Notebooks, office IT equipment, servers, and other IT equipment with proper RFI (Request for Information)/RFP (Request for Proposal) processes.

- Define contractual conditions for equipment maintenance, warranty, and post-warranty support with the chosen partners. Utilize the IT purchasing process and template to select reliable partners.

To effectively oversee external suppliers and partners, establishing robust relationships with the Purchasing team is imperative.

The Purchasing team plays a pivotal role in the IT procurement process, from vendor selection to contract negotiation and ongoing supplier management. Building strong relationships with Procurement fosters an environment of cooperation, where expectations are clearly communicated and aligned with organizational objectives.

7.2 HAVE KEY TECHNICAL KNOWLEDGE INSIDE YOUR TEAM.

To keep key knowledge and expertise internally, the IT Leader should:

- Develop in-house expertise to ensure control over systems, challenge partners effectively, and enhance service delivery.

- Create a team of professionals with knowledge in configuring, recovering from incidents, and managing systems, even if external partners handle most responsibilities.

real-life case about how full IT Outsourcing was leading to a big failure.

When I worked for an international company, one of our affiliates decided to outsource IT to an external vendor. (as the sub-chapter says "Keep your key staff inside the team" I'm personally and professionally totally against such an approach of fully outsourcing IT … but let's see what happened.)

The reasons were quite clear:
- Difficulty in finding and hiring good talents.

- Difficulty in maintaining the necessary number of specialists and certificates per system (due to many systems).
- Difficulty in properly maintaining the architecture (due to many systems).

Of course, the difficulty was mainly related to the cost of hiring, certifications, and retaining IT staff.

Even though the company was performing well with revenue and its position in the market, its IT costs were higher compared to other affiliates and the average IT costs vs. revenue KPI. The Financial pressure was huge, therefore they decided to 'almost' fully outsource IT to an external supplier, keeping internally on PM function!

After 5 years of IT outsourcing, the company's operations were in complete disarray regarding collaboration with IT. Almost nothing related to IT was under control.

What does it mean IT was not under control?

Marketing wants to implement some new offers or new products. Market in any domain has a lot of competition, therefore such projects to implement new things are very frequent, can be 50 to 100 per year or more.

If the company does not launch this kind of offers, services, and products, it is going to have a very hard time... because customers may leave and go to a competitor easily.

Imagine, from a business standpoint they are doing all needed for these projects, but when it comes to the IT, department which must deliver the project, it is becoming very difficult to get the clarity: what is the feasibility? what will be the timing of delivery? what will be the cost and impact on other offers?

Because of this unclear situation, almost all the teams and departments are suffering: not clear when Customer service is going to train their agents, not clear when Sales will train their staff, not clear when to work on the PR messages, not clear when finance needs to prepare and analyze the impact of the implemented project on the revenue, and so on.

Certainly, for a company reliant on IT-delivered services, this chaos has given rise to financial and marketing considerations as well.

After this experience of losing control over IT, they understood it was a mistake.

They finally decided to move back a significant part of IT responsibilities, internalizing a key part of IT.

Takeaway from this story: Every technology company must keep key IT/technology personnel internally. Some parts of IT may be outsourced, but control should be kept internally.

~~end of story~~

You might be wondering how to identify the knowledge that should be retained within the team.

Here is a practical way to determine which knowledge should be kept inside the IT team, based on my experience.

It is essential to maintain internal expertise in the following domains:

- **Used system software**: For any system software your team uses, such as Microsoft or Linux technologies, it's crucial to have in-house administration expertise, including all the versions in use. (Sys admins, DevOps, SREs)

- **Used databases**: For any database technology your team utilizes, you need to have internal knowledge of managing these databases. (DBAs)

- **Used hardware:** Knowledge of managing the hardware you use is necessary.

- **Used IT equipment:** Expertise in any other IT equipment should be maintained internally. You may need to engage additional resources from partners if you have a large quantity of equipment or if it's geographically distributed.

(note) Utilizing external partners for support of your various IT equipment does not eliminate the need for internal expertise.

- **Used business software (like Billing, CRM, ERP, HRM, etc.):** Primarily for configuration and support. If your company uses any business software, you need internal engineers trained to manage this software at the level provided by the supplier, at minimum for configuration and support.

(note) Some suppliers offer development capabilities within their systems. Whether to keep an internal team for development or to purchase development services from the supplier or its partners is a decision that depends on pricing, time to market, etc.

- **Cloud business software:** There are two scenarios for such software:
    - If the software is used completely independently, the IT team may not need any knowledge of this software.
    - If there is any integration with the software, the IT team will need to have someone internally responsible for managing the software and its integration part.

Why is it so important to maintain internal expertise in these key areas?

Let's see two practical cases described below: one involves an unprepared individual dealing with an incident that needed to be resolved with a partner, and the second case involves a person who was professionally prepared to handle the situation.

Case 1 (no expertise inside the team)

An issue arose with one of our services. The individual tasked with addressing the problem was not sufficiently trained and lacked a deep understanding of the system. They were unfamiliar with the location of the logs, the software version, and recent changes made to the system.

During the incident, this person contacted the support service of our partner, which provided these services. This person reported that the service was malfunctioning and requested assistance to restore it. However, the call lacked evidence and detail, leading the partner's support service to ask several questions, such as the software version, the database status, and the last time an upgrade, update, or patch was applied. Receiving no constructive responses, they requested that our engineer send an email with this detailed information.

This type of interaction resulted in additional time spent gathering the requested information. Instead of immediately addressing the issue, the partner requested further details. The situation was not urgent for them because they were awaiting a formal report of the issue, not just a call reporting a problem. Typically, it takes at least 15-30 minutes (sometimes up to an hour) to collect all the necessary information. Then providing the information late often led to back-and-forth communication, such as "Some information is missing" or "The provided information is insufficient." Consequently, the partner or supplier began addressing the issue later ranging from 15 minutes to an hour.

This meant that your customers could not use the system and its functionalities, while the supplier awaited further information instead of promptly dealing with the issue.

Case 2 (professional attitude and knowledge)

The second case highlights the importance of having the right expertise within the IT team.

Our engineers are responsible for all business applications. They are knowledgeable about versions and details (e.g., OS, Database), and they keep track of the last upgrades, updates, or patches applied, even if these actions were not performed by them. They monitor the software after any work is done by a supplier.

Now, imagine the same issue arises, and the system is not working. According to the Service Level Agreement (SLA), you need to call the supplier and send a Trouble Ticket (TT). The person responsible for the system, or your engineer, gathers all the necessary information—including versions, details, and the history of recent work—and sends the TT to the supplier.

Upon calling the supplier, this individual only needs to mention that there is an issue, and the details are included in the TT.

In this scenario, the supplier begins working on the TT immediately. Furthermore, if any information is missing from your ticket, they will not halt their investigation but will either check it themselves or ask your engineer for clarification.

So, how do you think the supplier's attitude in case 1 and case 2 will differ?

Obviously, in the first case, as the information is incomplete, the supplier spends time without a concrete case to solve.

In the second case, the supplier starts immediately and adopts a much more professional attitude towards resolving the issue.

The key takeaway from point 7.2 is - the importance of maintaining critical expertise within an IT team across various domains, including system software, databases, hardware, IT equipment, and business software (including cloud-based solutions).

Having this expertise not only ensures operational efficiency and effectiveness in managing and supporting these systems but also significantly impacts the team's ability to respond to and resolve incidents swiftly and effectively.

7.3 SELECTION OF PROPER ARCHITECTURE/ TECHNICAL SOLUTION

Technologies are constantly evolving: new solutions emerge, and existing ones gain new functions. How can you stay on top of these changes without being overwhelmed by innovation?

Implement a straightforward but rigorous process with strict requirements for selecting the appropriate architecture, technical solutions, innovative approaches or tools.

For example, each and any change in the architecture must be:

- Checked versus licensing compliance.
- Checked versus interoperability with all core elements and non-core but critical elements.
- Checked on a test environment.
- Validated by [create a list of validators].
- Modifications Communicated clearly with all the possible actions that must be done for the implementation and rollback.

The selection and approval process can involve various practices and tools.

One example is the SWOT analysis, which stands for Strengths, Weaknesses, Opportunities, and Threats. A SWOT analysis offers a high-level overview to aid in the decision-making process for selecting an IT solution, considering both internal capabilities and external possibilities. Refer to the example in Table 5 below.

Table 5. Example of SWOT analysis - select the IT tool XYZ.

SWOT analysis for implementing the Tool XYZ	
Strength	**Weaknesses**
- Customizability to fit specific business needs - Potential integration with existing systems - Can improve efficiency and productivity - Access to vendor support and updates	- Initial costs and potential for unexpected expenses - Time required for implementation and training - Risk of disruption during the transition period - Possible compatibility issues with existing infrastructure
Opportunities	**Threats**
- Ability to gain competitive advantage through improved operations - Access to new technologies and innovations - Potential to scale and adapt as the business grows - Opportunity to streamline processes and reduce manual work	- Changes in technology may render the solution obsolete - Risk of vendor lock-in and dependency - Security vulnerabilities and data privacy concerns - Potential resistance to change within the organization

While tools are not crucial for this process, they can enhance visualization and aid in making informed decisions. These include presentation tools (PowerPoint, Slides), documentation tools (Confluence, SharePoint), and various reporting tools (Excel, Sheets, BI solutions).

7.4 MONITORING TOOLS AND PROCESSES ARE MANDATORY

Incorporate monitoring tools to keep systems under control, detect issues promptly, and ensure proactive management.

Additionally, consider implementing alert mechanisms for real-time notifications, regularly analyze performance metrics to identify trends, and establish automated reporting for a comprehensive overview of system health.

A real-life story about the importance of proper Monitoring and cooperation of IT with the monitoring teams is presented in point 5.6.

Monitoring

Monitoring tools and KPIs are often assigned the lowest priority for implementation. Typically, most elements of production systems are implemented first. Then, usually only after the system launch, do monitoring systems begin to be considered—sometimes, they only become a priority following an incident.

I believe that monitoring tools should be an integral part of production systems by design and, therefore, ought to be implemented from day one, especially when managing real-time systems that are expected to operate 24/7.

Initially, monitoring can be somewhat limited, focusing on only the key elements. Over time, additional elements can be integrated to provide a more comprehensive view of your system's capacity and overall status.

It's crucial to track standard parameters such as CPU usage, RAM, disk space, disk activity (including read and write operations), network bandwidth, and network quality (for example, packet loss), as well as both internal and external network performance.

Additionally, service monitoring should be implemented to track standard customer activities. This holistic approach allows for the observation of IT systems from two perspectives: Technical and Functional.

Even if CPU and RAM usage appear stable, excessive disk activity could negatively affect database performance.

Similarly, all technical parameters might be within acceptable ranges, yet there could be no customer logins for an hour, for instance. In such scenarios, it's advisable to set up special alarms to check services like login.

Monitoring is also closely related to capacity planning. The architecture of the application itself is crucial and must be monitored—for example, if an application shifts some processes from disk to memory, this change should be monitored, and the outcomes assessed using monitoring tools.

Such modifications might speed up certain activities due to memory processing, but it's essential to consider whether your system is designed to handle this type of load.

Combining monitoring with testing is instrumental in determining whether changes in load affect service quality or not and impact the system capacity or not.

Capacity Management

Capacity planning is integral to numerous IT Leader's activities, including budgeting, purchasing, project implementation, considering architectural changes, integrating new platforms or APIs, and many others. Failure in this process can significantly impact your company, leading to financial losses, compromising your market position, and potentially infringing on business licensing regulations, especially if incidents violate license rules.

Therefore, it is recommended to incorporate considerations of capacity into all activities related to changes, planning, and budgeting—be it for a new project or a change initiative.

For instance, when discussing a new marketing idea with your team, include a few critical questions in your evaluation checklist: Will this impact system capacity? Could it increase usage in one or more systems? Even if the effects aren't immediately apparent, there might be an indirect influence on capacity. Recognizing this allows you to factor these considerations into your broader capacity planning and management activities.

Real-Life Story: The Consequences of Inadequate Capacity Planning

The primary system was supported by a powerful database server, whereas the standby server had significantly less processing power, more than halved.

Additionally, the database configurations for the main and standby servers differed.

A failure in the main server led to an uncontrollable situation: it began restarting frequently without an identifiable cause, resulting in a complete loss of service.

Faced with this, after a few hours of recovery attempts, we

decided to switch to the standby server, a risky move due to technology limitations at the time, which made reverting to the original server challenging.

The transition to the standby server resulted in severely slowed services. It took several hours of investigation—compounded by the team's exhaustion from extended hours of incident management—to discover that the database settings on the standby server were inadequately configured for the actual database load.

Adjusting the database parameters eventually stabilized the system sufficiently to maintain service until the main server was replaced by the supplier.

The total downtime experienced by customers was approximately 10 hours. Meanwhile, our team labored for over 36 continuous hours to resolve the incident.

Customer Service and retail locations were inundated with inquiries and visits from clients expecting uninterrupted service, leading to widespread frustration due to the inability to provide definitive answers about service restoration and compensation for the significant disruption.

The root cause was later identified as a hardware issue with one of the CPUs in the main server. While hardware failures are sometimes unavoidable, the incident underscored the necessity of eliminating Single Points of Failure. The prolonged incident duration was a direct result of inadequate contingency planning. Our reliance on the durability of hardware and software from reputable suppliers led to the oversight of adequately equipping and configuring the standby server.

At times, apprehension or self-confidence prevents us from insisting on redundant systems identical to the primary setup and allocating the necessary funds to ensure core business applications remain operational, even in the face of primary hardware failures.

~~ End of Story ~~

Modern configurations offer greater resilience through advanced protections, clusters, virtualization, and disaster recovery solutions.

However, this example serves as a reminder that failing to meticulously plan for contingencies and placing too much confidence in hardware and software reliability, can lead to failures with severe consequences for the businesses we support.

Monitoring tools

Monitoring tools play a crucial role in IT operations, ensuring systems are running optimally and efficiently. Here are some widely-used monitoring tools, along with use cases for each:

1. **Nagios**
   - **Use Cases**: Nagios is widely used for monitoring system performance, network protocols, applications, and server metrics. It's particularly useful for alerting IT staff about system failures, overloaded servers, or network connectivity issues.
2. **Zabbix**
   - **Use Cases**: Zabbix excels in network monitoring, server monitoring, and cloud monitoring. It's used for tracking network utilization, server load, and application performance, making it ideal for businesses needing comprehensive IT infrastructure monitoring.
3. **Prometheus**
   - **Use Cases**: Often used alongside Kubernetes,

Prometheus is great for monitoring time-series data. It's commonly employed for recording real-time metrics in a scalable way, alerting, and handling multi-dimensional data like labels or time series.

4. **Splunk**
    - **Use Cases**: Splunk is renowned for its ability to analyze and visualize large volumes of machine-generated data. It's widely used for security information and event management (SIEM), log management, and operational intelligence.

5. **Datadog**
    - **Use Cases**: Datadog provides cloud-scale monitoring for applications, networks, and servers. Its use cases include real-time performance tracking, cloud service monitoring across various platforms, and application performance management (APM).

6. **Grafana**
    - **Use Cases**: Grafana is often used for visualizing metrics from various data sources like Prometheus and InfluxDB. It's ideal for creating dashboards that display metrics through graphs and charts for real-time analysis.

7. **Dynatrace**
    - **Use Cases**: Dynatrace offers APM and cloud infrastructure monitoring, focusing on AI-powered insights. It's used for automatic problem detection, performance optimization, and digital experience monitoring, providing deep operational insights.

8. **New Relic**
    - **Use Cases**: New Relic specializes in APM and server monitoring, providing insights into application performance and user experiences. It's useful for businesses looking to optimize web applications, track errors, and analyze transaction data.
9. **SolarWinds**
    - **Use Cases**: SolarWinds is known for its network performance monitoring capabilities. Use cases include monitoring network device performance, fault detection, and network optimization to ensure reliable service delivery.
10. **Elastic Stack (ELK)**
    - **Use Cases**: Comprising Elasticsearch, Logstash, and Kibana, ELK is used for searching, analyzing, and visualizing log data in real-time. It's ideal for log analysis, security information and event management (SIEM), and operational troubleshooting.

Each of these tools offers unique features and capabilities, catering to different monitoring needs and use cases within the IT ecosystem.

7.5 REPORTING AND BI - MANAGE THEM PROPERLY

Why do I consider reporting and BI so important? When I began my role as an IT Manager, I noticed that reporting was often viewed as less 'cool' or glamorous compared to other IT and technology responsibilities. However, my experience working with business counterparts and understanding their expectations and processes gave me a clear insight: a company without effective reporting is like a 'clock without hands'. Even if the clock is renowned, aesthetically pleasing, and functions well internally, without 'hands' to show seconds, minutes, and hours, it will be perceived as broken and useless.

Implement a robust reporting and business intelligence strategy, emphasizing "common" approaches for information reporting. Insist on a unified understanding of key indicators across systems and reports, establishing a shared "one truth" layer.

For example, define what constitutes an active or inactive customer to align reporting metrics.

Real-case - an example of implementing a "one-truth" layer on top of our data.

The case itself is simple, but it was very challenging to execute.

One of my teams was responsible for developing and delivering reports and BI for the entire company.

We had a good process for handling reporting requests, and the team performed well in delivering reports and providing a BI solution for different business departments.

When a report was required, each business department had its KPIs (Key Performance Indicators), and its terminology, and even the understanding of KPIs was quite specific for each department.

And what happened was the following: once, when presenting to the CEO, one department was showing its figures/KPIs, and another department was presenting its figures/KPIs. What we, as IT, didn't see at the time was that when they (business colleagues) were presenting the figures to the CEO, they were using similar KPIs, BUT the figures were different!!!

Of course, it was not acceptable to have "incorrect" figures, so they addressed the issue to IT - asking why the figure was wrong. As you get it, the figures were not "incorrect," but the name of the KPI was similar to different figures.

After our internal analysis, we understood that even though they were using the "same terminology for their KPIs," the formulas they were using for one or another KPI were different.

Example: KPI - active customer

For Marketing, it meant: "a customer who is in an active phase, using services at least x times per month."

For IT, it meant: "a customer who is active in the system" (such a customer can be in any commercial status but is still incurring the license cost).

The problem was critical - reports and BI are used to decide on the next steps, and define the company's strategy! If the figures are not aligned - the strategy is impossible to follow and implement!

Therefore, a project was launched to:
- Define KPI names and formulas based on company needs.
- Agree on common terminology between departments.
- Have a BI and Reporting layer where all the data would be aggregated and located - used for most of the company's reporting.

One of the key points: the project was led by Finance, as they held the responsibility for the company's reporting.

(Note): the result of any project depends on who is leading it, and its responsibilities and commitment to this project.

After several months of analysis, discussions, and meetings, the final specifications of how the KPIs must be calculated, how they have to be visible, and how they have to be used were finalized.

Here I want to emphasize the importance of Interdepartmental communication and cooperation: in most cases, each department has its strategy and priorities. And they should be focused on reaching results.

When working with IT to request a software tool or report, they consider this as part of their "reaching their results" work. And they do not see the dependency of similar tools or reports globally on the whole company.

But it is visible by IT, by the IT Leader. Therefore, the role of the IT Leader is to communicate with all leaders of business departments and with the CEO to facilitate the implementation of interdepartmental interaction.

One case is reporting, another case can be a common ERP or CRM solution. The more departments communicate and cooperate, the more efficient the work of IT will be - delivering solutions that will be useful for the whole company is much better than delivering unique and scattered solutions for each department separately.

From the IT side, we were part of almost all the meetings to understand and be in line with what could be requested.

(Note): the key point of IT participation was the following: even if almost everything is possible on the IT side, everything has a cost. Our responsibility was to find an optimal and efficient way to get, process, and provide the data properly and on time.

Then we started the development of this layer, and in several months, it was ready.

The first month after launch brought fantastic results - the new layer brought clarity to most of the KPIs, figures, and reports used in the company by different departments.
The business was confidently using this data to build the Strategy and Roadmap.

Takeaway from this case: To be a data-driven company, it is crucial to invest in the definition of KPIs and define how the information is used to see the company results and how it is used to create the company strategy.

~~ *end of story* ~~

7.6 INFORMATION SECURITY

Information Security is not just a separate domain. Information Security must be an integral part of each component listed above, and much more.

If other domains may not impact the whole company, this domain is impacting and is impacted by each employee independent of where the employee works.

We've discussed the importance of Information Security measures in the Process Chapter, in point 5.2.

To implement and manage Information Security it is important to:

- Cooperate with the Information Security team (if such a team or Department exists).

- Cooperate with HR and prepare information security information regarding using company data, and company information resources.

- Prepare a comprehensive presentation with main Information Security points: password rules, access and sharing rules, email ethics, etc. to be part of the initial handbook provided to each employee.

7.7 MANAGE IT KPIS

The work of an IT Leader and the IT department overall is multifaceted, encompassing various levels or domains such as:
- Managing equipment
- Managing software
- Providing services to both internal and external clients
- Ensuring SLAs (Service Level Agreements) and effective Incident Management
- Promoting continuous learning
- Ensuring proper utilization of financial resources
- Among others...

To evaluate and demonstrate how the IT department is managing most of its responsibilities, as an IT Leader, you need to implement an IT KPIs (Key Performance Indicators) reporting system. This system should include the most important KPIs for both you and the company, calculate them, and present them.

Given that KPIs may vary across different companies or domains, I recommend following the logic of asking:
"Which services am I providing as IT?":
- If implementing projects, then project delivery KPIs should be included.
- If a budget is allocated to these projects, then a KPI for spending should be established.
- If providing a network for the company office, what is the network's availability?
- If responsible for the availability of production systems, what

is their availability?

This list is not exhaustive; it's merely an example to illustrate the logic.

To perform this exercise, you don't need a perfect list from other companies or industries. You can create your own KPIs list by following the simple logic mentioned above. Then, work on and analyze this list, implementing logical changes where needed. You may add some KPIs when you see a need.

It's crucial to have KPIs that focus on IT efficiency both internally and for Business.

Below is a table with examples of different KPIs, their descriptions, and value ranges.

Table 6. Example of IT KPIs.

#	KPI Name	Understanding	Expected Value
1	System Uptime	Measures the percentage of time IT systems are available and operational.	99.5% - 99.999%
2	Mean Time to Repair (MTTR)	The average time it takes to repair a system or component after a failure.	1-4 hours
3	Mean Time Between Failures (MTBF)	The average time between system failures.	300+ hours
4	First Call Resolution Rate	Percentage of incidents resolved during the first interaction with support.	70% - 90%
5	Help Desk Ticket Resolution Time	The average time it takes to resolve a help desk support ticket.	< 24 hours
6	Network Latency	The time it takes for a data packet to travel from source to destination.	< 150 milliseconds

7	Application Load Time	The time it takes for an application to become fully usable after launch.	< 2 seconds
8	Customer Satisfaction Score (CSAT)	Measures user satisfaction with IT services on a scale.	70% - 90%
9	IT Project Completion Rate	Percentage of IT projects completed on time.	85% - 95%
10	IT Budget Variance	The difference between the budgeted and actual IT spending.	±10%
11	Cost Per Ticket	The average cost of resolving a support ticket.	$15 - $50
12	Percentage of IT Budget Spent on Innovation	The portion of the IT budget allocated to new projects and innovation.	15% - 25%
13	Security Incidents per Year	The number of recorded security breaches or incidents per year.	0 - 5

As mentioned earlier, this KPI list is an example - you need to tailor them based on your IT team's responsibilities & services.

The expected values provided here are indicative and should be customized based on the organization's operational standards, industry benchmarks, and strategic objectives. Regular review and adjustment of these KPIs and their target values are crucial to ensure they remain aligned with the organization's evolving goals and challenges.

In summary, effective technology management involves a combination of internal and external collaboration, cultivating in-house expertise, selecting appropriate solutions, implementing monitoring tools, and establishing standardized reporting practices. These strategies collectively contribute to a well-managed and sustainable technology ecosystem.

Key Takeaways from Chapter 7: Manage Technology

Manage IT Borders Internally and Externally: Concentrate on defining clear roles for technology management within the company and with external partners, including the establishment of robust SLAs for each area.

Maintain Key Technical Knowledge In-House: Internal expertise is crucial for challenging partners and enhancing service delivery.

Rigorous Selection of Architecture/Technical Solutions: Implement a process with strict requirements for selecting appropriate technology solutions, including compliance checks, interoperability verification, and thorough testing before implementation.

Implement Monitoring Tools and Processes: Implement monitoring tools and establish alert mechanisms for early issue detection and proactive management, along with regular performance analysis to maintain the systems' health.

Standardize Reporting and Integrate Information Security: Develop a unified reporting and business intelligence strategy that aligns with company standards. Implement integrated information security standards.

Tailored IT KPI Reporting - Tailor your IT KPI reporting system. It aids in evaluating and demonstrating the effectiveness across various domains.

Your records: I encourage you to write down your conclusion, ideas, and actions from this Chapter. This action will ensure that the information you get will have practical utilization.

CHAPTER 8. MANAGE IT BUDGET

As highlighted in Chapter one, the IT budget is a pivotal tool enabling organizations to allocate resources effectively, prioritize initiatives, and ensure the IT department aligns with the technological needs of the business.

The budget for an IT department constitutes the financial plan encompassing anticipated expenses related to information technology functions within an organization. It spans various aspects of IT, encompassing hardware and software purchases, the acquisition of new software and licenses, infrastructure maintenance, personnel costs, training, cybersecurity measures, and other expenditures associated with managing and enhancing the organization's technological capabilities.

Given that IT Leaders typically lack a financial background, personal and organizational investments in knowledge are crucial for adept budget management.

Real-life Case: Failure in Budget Planning and Its Serious Impact.

This is a real-life case from my experience where a failure in proper budget planning led to a significant crisis affecting the company's operations.

Every year, one of our budget exercises involved capacity planning for the upcoming year. In our process, the business forecasted all relevant figures and technical teams conducted standard capacity planning exercises based on these projections. For equipment or software requiring upgrades, we meticulously planned the budget through multiple iterations, leaving no points unnoticed.

As described in this chapter, the budget was typically approved by the end of November. No changes were accepted after this point until the first budget review meeting.

Fast-forward to a hot summer day. I received a call from my team one Saturday reporting an issue in the data center—servers were shutting down due to problems with the air conditioning system. I, along with colleagues from various teams, rushed to the site to address the problem.

The company's services were down!

When company services are down, it becomes a highly stressful situation for all departments and the clients: stores are overwhelmed with customers inquiring when the issue will be resolved, and customer service is flooded with calls asking the same question. To add more complexity – people within the company are contacting each other to find out when and how this will be resolved. Some, more stressed than others, may start arguments, and so on.

Upon reaching the data center, we discovered that one of the three air conditioning systems had failed, and the remaining two were unable to maintain the required temperature. This caused the servers, including those hosting applications and databases, to automatically shut down due to overheating.

We improvised a solution by opening doors and introducing additional fans to cool the data center. After about an hour, the temperature began to drop, and we were able to restart the services. The faulty conditioning system was repaired later that day.

The incident lasted around 3 to 4 hours, significantly impacting our services and damaging the company's image. Post-recovery, we conducted an incident analysis, including a root cause analysis, and devised measures to prevent such incidents in the future.

What became evident was that this incident could have been avoided if the fourth air conditioning system had been purchased and installed before the summer began.

Upon reflection, we understood that the team responsible for planning the capacity of power and air conditioning systems failed to include the fourth system in the budget. Furthermore, during the first-quarter budget review in April, they once again overlooked its inclusion. In April, the issue was aggravated by the challenge of including something over budget during the review. Typically, securing approval for a budget increase required extensive discussions with the CEO and CFO, and this exercise was not conducted effectively. Their initial request to include the fourth air conditioning system during the budget review was declined, and unfortunately, they didn't pursue it further.

Takeaway from this story:

Properly conducting capacity management and budget planning exercises is crucial. Additionally, it's important to acknowledge personal mistakes and persist in pursuing necessary changes, even if the initial request faces obstacles. When each team conducts its responsibilities diligently and rectifies mistakes, the company will experience fewer incidents and issues, contributing to its overall success and financial well-being.

~~ end of story ~~

The budgeting process generally involves two main phases: Budget Planning and Budget Review.

Below we will examine each of them.

8.1 BUDGET PLANNING

As discussed in Chapter 3, a solid strategy forms the basis for effective budget planning. Following a well-constructed strategy, the subsequent step is budget development, requiring financial resources for both new initiatives and ongoing operational and support costs.

IT budgets usually have two primary categories:

- **CAPEX (Capital Expenditures):** Covers planned purchases of new infrastructure, licenses, systems, etc. Costs are estimated based on current expenses with a safety margin considering country-specific factors and historical price changes.

- **OPEX (Operational Expenditures):** Involving support contracts, SLAs, operational costs, training, and staff While costs are generally clearer than in CAPEX, collaboration with the Finance department is imperative for advice on pricing changes, exchange rate fluctuations, etc.

Budget planning typically starts three months before the year-end, with the final approval of the next year's budget around the end of November to early December.

During the budget planning exercise, the IT department receives capacity forecasts from various business departments. Subsequently, these figures are utilized to strategically plan the essential budgetary components for projects, capacity upgrades, supplier upgrades and updates, and other pertinent aspects.

8.2 BUDGET REVIEW

Regular quarterly checks of the budget are considered good practice. The budget planned for Q1 is scrutinized against real expenses, any variations are explained and re-planned, and the budget file is updated accordingly. Depending on market challenges, some budget parts may be adjusted or deferred during this process.

In certain instances, unforeseen investments may arise during budget reviews due to company situations and market challenges.

In conclusion, effective budget management is an integral aspect of an IT Leader's responsibilities.

Mismanagement can hinder the ability to provide expected solutions, maintain service levels, hire personnel, and provide necessary training and materials. Continuous monitoring of costs and collaboration with finance counterparts for regular updates on extra-budget, over-budget, and under-budget cases is essential for successful IT budget governance.

8.3 IT BUDGET DOMAINS

Let's now look at the possible items for an IT budget.

This table offers a general overview of how IT budget items can be categorized as CAPEX (Capital Expenditures) or OPEX (Operating Expenses).

Table 7. IT Budget - CAPEX.

CAPEX Domains	Short Description of Domains
Hardware Purchases	All IT equipment, from personal computers to Data center equipment (sometimes it may include mobile devices if they are used as IT equipment)
- Servers	
- Networking equipment	
- Storage devices	

- Personal computers and laptops	
- Mobile devices for employees	
Software Acquisitions	New Software acquisition of Customer software development
- One-time license purchases	
- Custom software development	
Building Infrastructure	All the infrastructure related to the Building and Datacenter
- Data center construction/modification	
- Cabling and networking infrastructure	
Major Software Upgrades	Upgrades of existing software that are not part of software monthly or yearly support.
- Large-scale software implementation	
Intangible Assets	Specific assets like Intellectual properly

PRACTICAL GUIDE FOR IT LEADERS

- Software patents and copyrights	
Project Specific Costs	here you can include all the projects from the Roadmap (Business and IT projects)
- Costs associated with major IT projects, not falling into yearly operational costs	

Now that we have an understanding of what is included in CAPEX, let's examine the main domains of OPEX in the IT budget:

Table 8. IT Budget - OPEX.

OPEX Domains	Short Description of Domains
Software Licenses (recurring fees)	All the payments which are monthly or yearly as part of your purchasing agreement
- Cloud Services (e.g., AWS, Azure)	
- SaaS subscriptions (e.g., Salesforce)	
Maintenance and Support Contracts	all the contracts of support and maintenance.
- Software support and updates	

189

- Hardware maintenance and repairs	
Utilities	Monthly services like Utilities, Internet service cost, Equipment maintenance
- Electricity for data centers/IT equipment	
- Internet service fees	
Salaries and Benefits	Salaries, Bonuses, Training cost of IT staff
- IT staff salaries	
- Training and professional development	
Cloud Services (operational usage)	Recurring cost of Cloud services
- Compute, storage, and data transfer costs	
Outsourcing Services	Specific services used to provide IT support.
- IT support and managed services	
- Consulting services	
Travel and Expenses	Travel and Expenses for

	work purposes (duty work, training)
- Travel related to IT operations, such as vendor meetings or training	

In some companies, the approach to cloud-based services or long-term licenses can be different. For example, all long-term cloud-based solutions, paid monthly or yearly, may then be capitalized, as they are considered part of your infrastructure.

Similarly, some software licenses might be capitalized if they provide benefits over several years and meet the organization's capitalization criteria.

8.4 THE STRATEGIC ESSENCE OF IT SPENDING

Typically, the IT budget constitutes a significant portion of the company budget.

Naturally, there are many questions from business leaders about why IT is so costly.

Therefore, it falls within the IT Leader's role to openly discuss with business managers in the company and explain precisely what each budget element entails, its cost, and the benefits the company derives from it.

Here are some fundamental principles concerning the IT budget and its value:

1. Digital Transformation and Innovation:
Businesses are constantly undergoing digital transformation to stay competitive. This involves the adoption of new technologies, processes, and business models. Innovation requires investment in cutting-edge technology, research and development, and new systems that can streamline operations, enhance customer experiences, and open new revenue streams. These initiatives are essential for growth but come with significant costs.

2. Infrastructure and Maintenance:

The backbone of any organization's IT capabilities is its infrastructure, which includes data centers, networks, servers, and cybersecurity measures. Building, maintaining, and regularly updating this infrastructure to ensure reliability, efficiency, and security represents a considerable portion of the IT budget. Additionally, as technology rapidly evolves, there's a continuous need for upgrades and replacements, adding to the expenses.

3. Software and Cloud Services:

Licensing fees for essential software, subscriptions to cloud services, and support contracts are recurring expenses that can accumulate to a significant portion of the budget. The shift towards cloud computing, while offering scalability and flexibility, involves operational costs related to data storage, processing, and software-as-a-service (SaaS) subscriptions, which can be substantial depending on the size and needs of the business.

4. Compliance and Security:

With increasing threats from cyberattacks and the need for compliance with various regulatory standards (e.g., GDPR - General Data Protection Regulation in the EU, HIPAA - Health Insurance Portability and Accountability Act, a US law), businesses must invest heavily in cybersecurity measures. This includes sophisticated security software, regular security audits, training for employees, and possibly hiring dedicated security personnel or consultants. The cost of ensuring data privacy and security is a significant and non-negotiable expense in the IT budget.

5. Human Capital:

Skilled IT professionals are in high demand and command high salaries. Investing in a talented workforce to manage, support, and innovate within the IT landscape is crucial. This includes not only the salaries but also benefits, training, and professional development to keep the skills of the IT staff up to date. Additionally, as IT projects become more complex and integral to every aspect of the business, the need for more specialized personnel increases, further driving up costs.

These factors combined underscore the strategic importance of the IT Budget for operational support, competitive advantage, and future growth. As technology continues to evolve and integrate more deeply into all aspects of business operations, the IT budget reflects both the opportunities and the necessities of this digital age.

8.5 BUDGET AND DAY-TO-DAY ACTIVITIES

In this chapter, we've discussed the essence of the IT Budget, including its components, the main processes of preparing and reviewing the budget and taking a strategic view of the IT Budget.

I now aim to enhance the practical application of the IT budget in actions undertaken by IT management and teams. In many companies, there's a common misconception that the budget process is an external and complex requirement - something done because it must be done, while the rest of the time work proceeds as if there's no budget consideration. In reality, budget and financial planning is part of any activity we are doing as IT Leaders.

How does the budget intersect with our day-to-day tasks and activities?

Let's explore a few actions common for any IT Leader.

The first activity to consider is: The Maintenance of IT Infrastructure and Software

We've touched already on activities linked with capacity management, monitoring, and operational activities in several chapters.

IT Infrastructure

To maintain IT infrastructure effectively, we need to consider important elements:

- **Power**: It's often necessary to have redundant power sources to ensure equipment functions properly despite power issues. This might include additional power sources, and power protections like UPSes, which require their maintenance.

Effectively, maintaining IT infrastructure demands significant planning practices that directly require financial planning.

- **Cabling**: Quality equipment and software are ineffective without investment in a good cabling system. This affects the reachability of our software for business and IT monitoring. Investing in quality cabling and selecting the right category for your IT & office infrastructure implies financial planning.
- **Cooling**: Given that equipment consumes and generates significant heat, investment in a reliable conditioning system is crucial for maintaining IT systems. Planning and managing cooling also involves financial planning.

Software Maintenance

Standard practices related to software maintenance include (but are not limited to):

- **Support from Suppliers**: For software that must operate 24/7, SLAs with suppliers are essential. Managing these agreements properly requires financial planning to define the SLA terms, costs, and protections offered and financial review to verify if the applied services are well applied according to the allocated budget.
- **Software Upgrades**: Some software updates and upgrades are available only with a maintenance

or warranty contract. Regular financial planning and reviews are necessary to ensure continuous software operation.

Another activity to consider is "Build or Buy"

When faced with projects or business requirements not covered by existing IT solutions, we encounter the "Build or Buy" dilemma.

Building solutions internally is often perceived as a cheaper and faster option. However, when considering the long-term perspective, is it truly the best scenario in terms of business and financial outcomes? Let's see the comparison below.

Building Internally Includes:

- **People to Describe It**: Naturally, you need someone to draft requirements. However, when the development is entirely internal, specifications often change along the way without corresponding updates to the documentation. This can result in a functional product whose documentation and requirements are outdated, complicating future migrations or the addition of new functionalities.
- **People to Prepare the Architecture, Capacity, Budget, Resources, Teams**: Building internally encompasses the entire architecture, including database and server architectures and the selection of development languages. While it may seem straightforward initially, it's crucial to consider the implications 1 year or 5 years into the future.
- **People to Build It**: As mentioned, this requires dedicated personnel who can focus on the project without being distracted by other tasks, aiming for tangible results within a specific timeframe. A critical aspect of planning, especially financial planning, is considering the future availability

of these team members. What happens if key personnel leave within the next 3-5 years?
- **People to Maintain It, Long-Term, and Beyond**: Internal development means setting up all processes, including alarms, monitoring, responses, SLAs, change management, and problem management, in-house. It also involves preparing and delivering training for those who will maintain the product in the long run.

Financial Planning Considerations: The financial aspect of internal development can be somewhat unpredictable. Even with a well-assessed risk strategy, being solely responsible may lead to unforeseen errors and inevitable overspending. If you embark on this path, you might find it challenging to halt progress, even in the face of significant issues.

Buying Solutions Include:
- **People to Describe It**: Concentrate on defining key functionalities and choosing the best company that aligns with your requirements. Develop the necessary processes and contractual obligations detailing how the product will be delivered and changes implemented. Financial planning becomes significantly clearer, anchored to the supplier's commitments.
- **People to Prepare the Architecture, Capacity, Budget, Resources, Teams**: Selection of the supplier and partner is crucial. Subsequently, the responsibility for architecture, capacity, budgeting, resourcing, and team assignments lies with the supplier, albeit under your supervision. Your role entails ensuring the architecture's sustainability and compliance with all necessary functional and non-functional requirements, and confirming that financial planning is both agreed upon and

validated.
- **People to Build It**: The supplier has already constructed the product and may incorporate additional functionalities based on your specifications. They are responsible for documenting these additions and providing corresponding training. The supplier must also prepare documentation if it's specified in your requirements.
- **People to Maintain It, Long-Term, and Beyond the Present**: The supplier is obligated to ensure all necessary integration, alerting, and monitoring systems are in place. They must also furnish training materials and conduct the training as specified in your contract.

Financial Planning Considerations: the "Buy" process offers greater predictability. The supplier is bound by contractual obligations to maintain their software and platform. As the client, your responsibilities include making regular payments for the supplier's services, as outlined in your contract.

My Recommendations on Building Internally vs. Buying: In most cases today, I recommend purchasing the solution. However, there are specific scenarios where you might need to consider building internally:
- **Innovative Requirements**: If your requirements are entirely new, presenting a novel idea you prefer not to share with external suppliers, then you might opt to develop the solution internally. This way, you could potentially become the supplier of this innovative solution.
- **Proprietary Products**: If the project is your product that you intend to build, use, and potentially sell, you effectively become the supplier. In such cases, internal development is necessary.

- **Integration Needs**: Should you require specific integration elements that extend an existing platform, leveraging APIs to create your value-added services may be the way forward. Often, these functionalities entail significant costs when outsourced, as they fall outside the core offerings of most suppliers, who may then charge you for the full scope of development and support.

Another Activity: "Projects and Changes"

Before initiating a project or implementing a change, conducting a feasibility analysis is essential.

This analysis should assess:
- The complexity of the project
- The duration of the project
- The expected deadline

As an IT Leader, it is crucial to establish a process where feasibility is determined and provided through various scenarios, like in the example below:
- **Scenario 1**: Undertaken by an internal team with a duration of 2 months before user acceptance (UA) tests. This requires 3 personnel to be allocated, and it will impact Project Y.
- **Scenario 2**: Completed by an external supplier, with a duration of 3 weeks before UA tests. This scenario necessitates the allocation of 1 person for IT acceptance tests, with a preliminary cost of USD 10k.
- **Scenario 3**: Executed partially by both the internal team and an external supplier, lasting 5 weeks before UA tests. This involves 3 personnel and a budget of USD 5k.

Scenarios 1 and 2 are recommended. Scenario 3 might pose deadline risks (e.g., a potential 1-week delay due to integration issues).

Providing such analysis is vital for business and budgetary considerations for the project. If no budget is allocated, you might need to exclude Scenarios 2 and 3 or request additional funds.

This approach highlights a direct link between Strategy, Roadmap, and Budget: A robust strategy and execution roadmap enable you to daily secure the necessary budget and successfully implement what is required for your company's success.

Another Practice: "Staff Management"

Budget planning is inherently linked with team management.

Let's delve into key facets of managing a team:
- **Hiring**: You can proceed with hiring if there is a vacancy with a designated budget for a specific role. It's not feasible to hire a senior expert if the budget is set for a junior expert's salary.
- **Salaries and Bonuses**: Financial planning must cover all team salaries. Typically, employees anticipate salary increases every 6-12 months. Inadequate planning can lead to a lack of salary growth and demotivation. This excludes situations where financial constraints temporarily prevent salary increases or bonuses. If a bonus system is in place, employees will expect bonuses to reflect their performance.
- **Training and Conferences**: Allocate budget for training on new technologies, for onboarding new staff, and for updating existing software. Consider also budgeting for advanced training for key

personnel, which might involve higher costs for training, travel, and accommodation. Participation in industry conferences can serve as both a knowledge-sharing opportunity and a motivational tool for senior and key team members.
- **Investing in New Technologies**: As technology continuously evolves, investment in training and literature is essential to keep pace.

In this subsection, we learned about everyday practices and their integration with budget strategies. While not exhaustive, this overview, based on established practices, illustrates the integration with the budget process, ensuring financial support for projects, software, maintenance, or personnel is adequately planned and executed.

Key Takeaways from Chapter 8: Manage IT Budget

Effective IT budget management is crucial for aligning technological capabilities with organizational goals and ensuring optimal resource allocation.

A comprehensive understanding of both CAPEX and OPEX expenditures is essential for IT Leaders to navigate financial planning within the IT domain.

Proactive budget planning and regular review processes enable organizations to adapt to changing needs and market conditions efficiently.

Collaboration between IT and finance departments is vital for accurate forecasting and managing unexpected expenses within the allocated budget.

Continuous investment in digital transformation, infrastructure, software, security, and human capital is key to maintaining competitive advantage and supporting business growth.

The budget is a crucial aspect of an IT Leader's daily activities. Factoring in the budget for all tasks enables more effective financial planning and enhances the management of key IT Leaders' responsibilities.

Your records: I encourage you to write down your conclusion, ideas, and actions from this Chapter. This action will ensure that the information you get will have practical utilization.

CHAPTER 9. PROJECT MANAGEMENT METHODOLOGY

In this chapter, I want to address an important subject: Project Management methodologies and which is best for your case.

Choosing the right project management methodology for specific projects is a critical responsibility for IT Leaders, as it significantly impacts the successful implementation of changes and projects, essential for company development.

A stable IT solution with excellent SLAs is insufficient for the

IT Leader's responsibilities. If projects are not delivered on time, with the right quality, and using appropriate methodologies, it will pose a significant challenge for the company.

To start the selection of the right methodology and tools, IT Leaders need to consider which methodologies their team is familiar with, identify any issues with currently used methodologies for project implementation, and propose which methodology best suits each project.

Usually, the methodology of Project Management is part of the PMO's responsibility. Hence, the IT Leader, responsible for project delivery, should closely cooperate with the PMO to adapt or change existing PM methodologies for the best efficiency and delivery.

Waterfall or Agile?

What I don't personally like is the usual presentation of Agile vs. Waterfall - many times it is considered in the following way: Agile is a new methodology, a more contemporary one, while Waterfall is an old methodology that is obsolete.

This interpretation is completely wrong.

It's important to understand that Waterfall and Agile are not competitors but complementary approaches, with some projects better suited to Waterfall and others to Agile.

Let's do a short review of each Methodology (information taken from standard PM manuals).

9.1 WHAT IS THE WATERFALL METHODOLOGY?

The Waterfall methodology is a traditional project management approach that follows a linear and sequential design process. It is characterized by a strict phase-by-phase progression where each phase must be completed before the next one begins, with little to no overlap between phases.

In Picture 5 there is a representation of Waterfall methodology.

Waterfall model

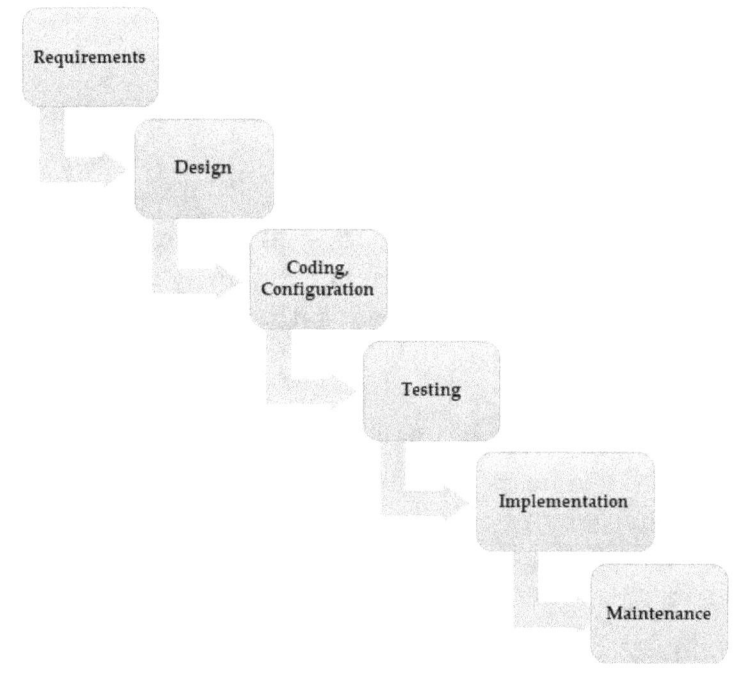

Picture 5. Diagram of Waterfall methodology

Key Characteristics of the Waterfall Methodology:

1. **Sequential Phases:** The Waterfall methodology divides the project into distinct phases such as Requirements, Design, Implementation (or Coding), Testing, Deployment, and Maintenance. Each phase relies on the deliverables of the previous phase and corresponds to a specialization of tasks.

2. **Detailed Documentation:** Because of its linear approach, the Waterfall methodology requires comprehensive documentation upfront. Each phase has its documentation requirements,

ensuring a clear and detailed plan before moving on to the next phase.

3. Well-defined Objectives: The scope, timelines, and costs of the project are clearly defined at the beginning. This makes the Waterfall methodology suitable for projects with well-understood requirements that are unlikely to change during the development process.

4. Limited Client Involvement: In a traditional Waterfall project, client or end-user involvement is typically concentrated at the beginning (during requirement gathering) and at the end (during acceptance testing) of the project.

5. No Going Back: Once a phase has been completed, the project moves to the next phase without revisiting or revising the previous phases. This makes it difficult to accommodate changes or new requirements without significant rework and cost implications.

As we have learned the main characteristics of the Waterfall methodology, let's now see what the usual phases are.

Phases of the Waterfall Methodology:

1. Requirements: This initial phase involves gathering and documenting all specific requirements of the project, outlining what the end product should achieve.

2. Design: Based on the requirements, this phase involves creating the system design. It can be divided into two parts: high-level system architecture and detailed design.

3. Implementation (Configuration, Coding, Installation): During this phase, developers write code based on the previously defined design documentation.

4. Testing: Once the software is developed, it undergoes thorough testing to find and fix any defects or issues.

5. Deployment: After testing, the product is released to the production environment or delivered to the customer.

6. Maintenance: Post-deployment, this phase involves making updates, fixing bugs, and adding enhancements to ensure the product continues to meet user needs.

The Waterfall methodology is known for its simplicity and ease of management, particularly in projects with clear objectives and stable requirements. However, its rigidity can be a drawback in dynamic environments where requirements are subject to change.

9.2 WHAT IS AGILE METHODOLOGY?

Agile methodology is an iterative and incremental approach to project management and software development that helps teams deliver value to their customers faster and with fewer headaches.

In Picture 6 there is a representation of Agile methodology.

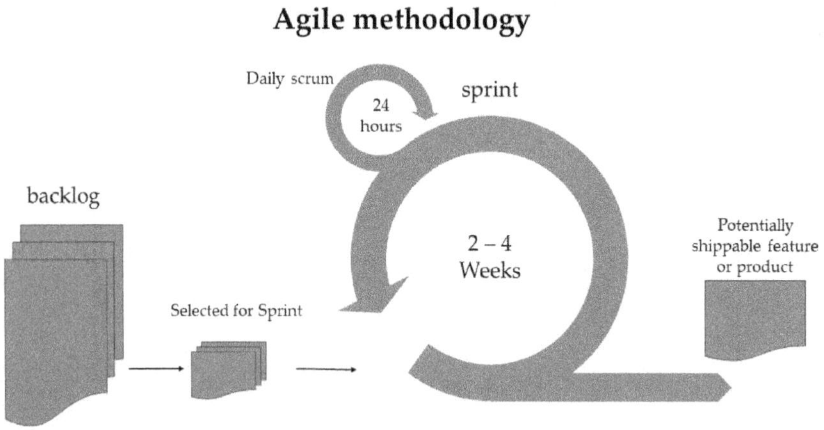

Agile methodology

Picture 6. Diagram of Agile methodology.

Key Characteristics of Agile Methodology are:

1. Iterative and Incremental Approach: Agile projects are divided into small, manageable units called iterations or sprints, which typically last between one to four weeks. Each iteration involves planning, designing, coding, and testing, resulting in a working product increment.

2. Customer Collaboration: Agile places a strong emphasis on customer involvement throughout the development process. Regular feedback is sought to ensure the product meets the customer's needs and expectations, allowing for adjustments as the project evolves.

3. Embrace Change: Agile methodologies welcome changing requirements, even late in development. Agile processes harness change for the customer's competitive advantage.

4. Cross-functional Teams: Agile projects are executed by self-organizing, cross-functional teams that collaborate closely. These teams encompass all the skills necessary to deliver product increments, from development to deployment.

5. Continuous Improvement: Agile methodologies encourage regular reflection on how to become more effective and then tuning and adjusting behavior accordingly. This applies to both the product and the process.

6. Simplicity: The art of maximizing the amount of work not done is essential. Agile methodologies emphasize simplicity and the importance of focusing on what's crucial to delivering value to the customer.

For IT Leaders, it is important to guide the PMO and IT team to choose the right methodology for a particular type of project: the key is "tailoring" the chosen methodology—Agile or Waterfall—to the project's needs and ensuring the project team fully understands the reasons behind the choice.

This involves a detailed consideration of project requirements, uncertainty levels, and the need for iterative development or a sequential approach.

Agile methodologies, characterized by sprints and iterative development, are recommended for projects with high uncertainty or those requiring frequent updates and functionality changes, like apps or platforms.

Conversely, projects with clear requirements and lower uncertainty levels may benefit more from the Waterfall methodology.

IT Leaders must ensure their teams are well-informed about the methodologies and possess the necessary skills to implement them effectively. This may involve training sessions, workshops, or bringing in external expertise.

Ultimately, the choice between Agile and Waterfall should not be seen as a binary one. Instead, IT Leaders should focus on selecting the best approach based on the specific needs of each project, even considering hybrid models that combine elements of both methodologies.

9.3 WHICH METHODOLOGY TO USE?

At the end of the Chapter, I would like to show as a general guide which projects are using Agile and which Waterfall (within the IT scope):

Table 9. A general guide for PM methodology usage.

Waterfall Projects	Agile Projects
Infrastructure Upgrades	**Software Development with Frequent Updates**
Upgrading network infrastructure or moving to a new data center requires careful planning and execution in a linear fashion.	Developing a web application or mobile app where features and requirements evolve based on user feedback.
Legacy System Migrations	**E-Commerce Platform Development**
Migrating from an old mainframe system to a modern platform needs detailed upfront planning to ensure data integrity and system compatibility.	Building and iterating on an e-commerce platform that needs to adapt quickly to changing market demands or consumer preferences.
Compliance and Regulatory Projects	**Customer Relationship Management (CRM) Systems**
Implementing systems or processes to meet new	Developing or customizing CRM software to suit the

regulatory requirements often follows a strict sequence of steps to ensure compliance.	dynamic needs of sales and marketing teams, requiring frequent updates.
Large-Scale Construction IT Projects	**Agile Software Development Projects**
Implementing IT infrastructure in new buildings or campuses, where the project scope and requirements are well-defined, and changes are minimal.	Projects that involve developing software solutions with iterative feedback loops, such as mobile applications or SaaS products.
ERP Implementations	**Digital Marketing Platforms**
Enterprise Resource Planning (ERP) system implementations are large and complex, requiring extensive planning and a phased rollout.	Creating and iterating on digital marketing platforms or campaigns that need to respond quickly to analytics and market trends.
Disaster Recovery Planning	**Prototype or MVP Development**
Developing and implementing disaster recovery plans for IT systems, where all steps need to be meticulously planned and documented.	Developing a prototype or Minimum Viable Product for a new tech product or service to validate concepts in a real-world environment quickly.
Hardware Deployments	**User Experience (UX) Projects**
Rolling out new hardware across an organization, such as servers or workstations, often requires a sequential approach to ensure compatibility and minimize disruptions.	Iterative design and testing of user interfaces for software products, where user feedback is integral to the development process.

Key Takeaways of Chapter 9: Choosing the Right Project Management Methodology

Critical Decision for IT Leaders: Avoid selecting a methodology solely based on external influences. Consider internal factors like the team's familiarity with methodologies, existing methodological challenges, and suitability for specific projects. Offer ongoing support and training to enhance knowledge and practical skills.

Tailoring Methodologies (Waterfall, Agile, Hybrid): Ensure your team understands the core aspects of each methodology and involves them in choosing and customizing the most appropriate one for each project.

Your records: I encourage you to write down your conclusion, ideas, and actions from this Chapter. This action will ensure that the information you get will have practical utilization.

CHAPTER 10. TECHNOLOGIES TRANSFORMING THE IT LANDSCAPE

In this book, we've talked about very important topics like Strategy, Technology, Processes, Team, and Budgeting, which are key for anyone leading in IT. Getting them right is crucial for building strong IT support that helps businesses grow.

Having a strong foundation allows us to plan for the future practically.

In this part of the book, I want to highlight three big trends that are changing the world of IT soon. For some businesses, these changes might happen slowly, but for others, they're already happening.

These three important trends are:
- Planning your use of Cloud computing
- Following a Green IT strategy
- Using AI (Artificial Intelligence) to get ahead

No matter what kind of business you have, it's important to start using these trends as soon as you can. All businesses are now looking at being more sustainable, efficient, and quick.

As telecommunication gets better, offering us faster speeds and less delay, we have a chance to change our IT solutions. We can pick solutions and places that work better and are more efficient and improve the resilience of our systems without spending a lot on infrastructure.

Let's look at each trend one by one and talk about how they can benefit us, what challenges they might bring, and what good results we can expect.

10.1 CLOUD STRATEGY

To introduce the topic of cloud computing, let's start with a brief description:

Cloud computing is the provision of **computing services**—including servers, storage, databases, networking, software, analytics, and intelligence—over the Internet ("the cloud"). This approach offers faster innovation, flexible resources, and economies of scale.

It enables users to access and store data and applications on remote servers managed by cloud service providers, as opposed to personal computers or local servers. Essentially, cloud computing allows businesses and individuals to use applications without installation and to access personal files from any computer with internet access, significantly enhancing efficiency, data security, resource scalability, and cost-effectiveness.

Consider how, just a few years ago, we had to implement everything within our data centers. Now, when in need of a robust Project Management tool, the shift has moved towards cloud systems. These systems allow remote access from anywhere, on any device, simply by choosing a plan and paying for the features and the number of users.

In terms of computing power, contrast the traditional method of acquiring new IT solutions—which involved purchasing new equipment, installation, configuring OS and databases, and setting up IT and Business solutions—with the present, where such solutions were often overestimated for potential growth, consuming more resources than used.

Now, many of these steps can be either optimized or bypassed. For instance, to pilot a project, we can "rent" infrastructure in the Cloud, or even a database without worrying about the hardware behind it, install the necessary Business and IT solution, and launch it to a limited number of clients, choosing high availability and backup options directly within the Cloud solution.

Even if equipment purchase is necessary, initiating in the Cloud can expedite delivery. Once we have a functioning product, the process of buying equipment will not hold back the launch.

Today, cloud solutions are categorized into three main types based on their deployment model:

1. **Public Cloud**: Services are provided over the public internet and are available to anyone interested. Resources are owned and operated by third-party providers like AWS, Microsoft Azure, and Google Cloud Platform.
2. **Private Cloud**: Dedicated to a single organization, it can be hosted on-premises or by a third party, offering greater control and privacy.
3. **Hybrid Cloud**: A mix of public and private clouds, sharing data and applications between them to offer flexibility in moving workloads as needed.

Furthermore, cloud solutions are classified based on service models into:
- **Infrastructure as a Service (IaaS)**
- **Platform as a Service (PaaS)**
- **Software as a Service (SaaS)**
- **Function as a Service (FaaS)**

These distinctions help us understand the variety of cloud computing services available, each serving different organizational needs and goals.

As an IT Leader, developing your Cloud strategy is imperative.

Here's how to approach it practically:
- For every new project, analyze the possibility of using Cloud solutions first. Consider cost, technology availability, integration points, regulations, and security. If these factors align with a Cloud solution, proceed.
- For existing IT systems and services, evaluate the migration strategy carefully. Beyond financial calculations, consider the long-term benefits for the business.
- Encourage your team to train in Cloud vs. Datacenter technologies. Preparing your solutions for Cloud architecture, even if migration isn't immediate, will facilitate an easier transition later.
- Explore Cloud-based backup strategies. Storing large amounts of data in the Cloud can be efficient and forward-thinking.
- Utilize the Cloud for data analytics. Many companies use Cloud-based solutions for BI and reporting without needing to build complex infrastructure.
- Prioritize Business solutions available in the Cloud. For new system implementations like HRM or CRM, explore Cloud solutions first, possibly running pilot projects to assess compliance with your needs and requirements.

You might wonder: "How do I start? What if I encounter challenges? Are there any examples within my domain?"

Here are some examples of different companies using Cloud solutions for their projects and operations:

1. **Netflix**: A leading streaming service that relies on

cloud computing, specifically Amazon Web Services (AWS), to host its vast content library and deliver it to millions of users globally. This enables Netflix to efficiently manage demand surges and scale resources dynamically.

2. **Spotify**: Utilizes Google Cloud Platform (GCP) to handle its massive data processing and analytics needs. This supports Spotify's personalized music recommendation engine and overall user experience.

3. **Dropbox**: Originally hosted on AWS, Dropbox later moved to build its cloud infrastructure but still uses AWS for certain international customers. This transition allowed Dropbox to customize its cloud environment to better meet its file storage and sharing service needs.

4. **Adobe**: Adobe Creative Cloud is a SaaS offering that provides access to its creative software suite over the Internet. By transitioning to the cloud, Adobe has been able to offer a more flexible and scalable service model to its users.

5. **Capital One**: In the financial services sector, Capital One has been a pioneer in adopting cloud technology, specifically AWS, to enhance its customer banking experience, improve operational efficiency, and innovate in financial services.

6. **Airbnb**: Uses AWS to host its website and backend services. This cloud infrastructure supports Airbnb's global accommodations marketplace by providing the scalability needed to handle peak booking times and the analytics tools to understand user behavior.

7. **Toyota**: Utilizes Microsoft Azure for its Toyota Connected service, which leverages a wide range of cloud-based services to enhance the driving experience through data analytics from connected

vehicles.

8. **Zalando**: Europe's leading online fashion platform uses AWS to operate its digital storefronts and backend systems. The cloud enables Zalando to process high volumes of transactions and efficiently manage its supply chain.
9. **General Electric (GE)**: Uses AWS and Azure for its Predix platform, which supports industrial Internet of Things (IoT) applications, enabling predictive maintenance and analytics for industrial equipment.
10. **Johnson & Johnson**: Utilizes AWS to accelerate its software development for medical devices and to enable advanced healthcare platforms that can process and analyze vast amounts of data for better patient care.
11. **Siemens**: Leverages AWS and Siemens MindSphere, a cloud-based, open IoT operating system, to analyze vast amounts of data generated by industrial machines, thereby optimizing operations and manufacturing processes.
12. **Pfizer**: Uses cloud computing for drug discovery and development processes. The company relies on AWS and Google Cloud for high-performance computing tasks necessary for biochemical simulations and data analysis.
13. **HSBC:** One of the world's largest banking and financial services institutions, HSBC uses Google Cloud to drive its digital transformation, improve analytics, and enhance the customer banking experience.
14. **BMW**: Employs Microsoft Azure for its BMW ConnectedDrive service, which offers a range of digital services and features to enhance the driving experience through cloud-based navigation, information, and entertainment services.

15. **Unilever**: The global consumer goods company uses AWS to power its digital marketing platforms, improve supply chain efficiency, and harness data analytics for better consumer insights and product development.
16. **The New York Times**: Utilizes Google Cloud to digitize its vast archive of historical photos. The cloud's AI and machine learning capabilities help categorize, archive, and make the photos searchable.
17. **Shell**: Leverages Microsoft Azure to drive its digital transformation across all areas of business, from exploration and production of oil and gas to customer service initiatives at its retail locations.
18. **Duolingo**: The popular language-learning platform uses AWS to host its applications and data, enabling it to scale seamlessly to accommodate millions of users worldwide while personalizing learning content with AI and machine learning.

These real examples showcase the versatility and transformative potential of cloud services across a broad spectrum of industries, from healthcare and finance to manufacturing, retail, and education.

I believe it serves as good evidence to focus now on your Cloud strategy, if not done yet, and establish the future of your company through new innovative cloud solutions.

10.2 GREEN IT

Let's explore Green IT or sustainable computing, which emphasizes practices aimed at enhancing the environmental sustainability of technology use. This includes efforts to reduce energy consumption, minimize waste, and promote recyclability.

As IT leaders, embracing this challenge and initiating optimization programs is essential. Our leadership role extends to bettering the ecological situation in our nations by optimizing power resource expenditure and the efficient use of available resources.

Green IT transcends mere IT actions. Various business sectors are integrating the Green formula into their strategies, necessitating IT's adherence to new operational standards. The era of increasing equipment reliance, based solely on supplier offerings, is over. We must urge suppliers to deliver more efficient solutions.

Major corporations have already formulated strategies for more sustainable resource utilization, including investing in alternative power sources and adopting optimized, less consumptive solutions. Cloud solutions present one such beneficial opportunity.

Consider a company with multiple affiliates: a cloud solution could streamline IT resource utilization by providing a singular solution for all affiliates, such as HR software, ERP, or Project Management systems. Instead of maintaining separate, costly, and complex solutions for each affiliate, consolidating them into a single solution can significantly optimize resources like CPU, RAM, and storage. Individual solutions for each entity necessitate surplus hardware capacity, which cumulatively results in considerable wasted capacity across affiliates. A unified solution, however, utilizes a shared "safety margin" more efficiently.

Additional Green IT elements include (but are not limited to):
- **Energy-Efficient Servers**: Designed for peak energy efficiency, these servers incorporate advanced power management and low-power processors to decrease energy use without sacrificing performance.
- **Advanced Cooling Solutions**: Technologies like liquid cooling and free air cooling replace traditional cooling methods, reducing energy demands.
- **Virtualization and Consolidation**: This enables running multiple virtual machines on a single server, enhancing resource utilization and diminishing the need for excess hardware.
- **Renewable Energy Solutions**: Integration with renewable energy sources, such as solar or wind, supports eco-friendly data center operations.
- **Modular and Scalable Infrastructure**: Adaptable data center solutions ensure that resources match demand accurately, avoiding energy waste from unused equipment.
- **Software for Energy Management**: Tools for optimizing data center operations offer features for automated energy management and real-time environmental impact monitoring.

Adopting these strategies not only lessens environmental impact but also yields cost benefits through enhanced energy efficiency.

Here are some pertinent regulatory documents related to Green

IT:

- **Energy Efficiency Standards**:
    - **Energy Star**: Launched in 1992, it's a program by the U.S. EPA and Department of Energy.
    - **EU's Ecodesign Directive**: Initiated in 2009 to set efficiency requirements for various products.
- **Carbon Footprint Reduction**:
    - **Kyoto Protocol** and **Paris Agreement**: International agreements set to reduce carbon emissions.
    - These frameworks encourage IT practices that align with sustainability goals, including the adoption of cloud computing for its energy efficiency.
- **Data Center Regulations**: Certain areas provide guidelines or certifications aimed at improving data center energy efficiency.
- **Green Public Procurement (GPP)**: Government policies favor the procurement of eco-friendly IT products and services, focusing on energy efficiency and recyclability.

Navigating the complex landscape of Green IT regulations requires staying informed and proactive in sustainable IT practices, thereby supporting not just compliance but also contributing to wider environmental and social sustainability goals.

10.3 AI TECHNOLOGY

In recent years, it has become good practice to employ ML (Machine Learning) and AI (Artificial Intelligence) across many technological fields.

Even if we are satisfied with the current technology within our company, beginning to learn about AI tools and their use cases will aid in enhancing our future.

I aim to highlight some areas where AI has significant utility, accompanied by real examples.

Prediction Based on Historical Data:
- **Decision Support Based on Historical Data**
    - **Automated Data Insights**: AI can analyze extensive datasets to uncover trends, patterns, and insights, informing better decision-making.
    - **Predictive Analytics**: With AI's help, companies can predict future trends from historical data, aiding in strategic planning and resource allocation.
- **Enhancing Customer Experiences**
    - **Personalization**: AI can customize customer experiences by analyzing behaviors, preferences, and past interactions.
    - **Chatbots and Virtual Assistants**: Deploying AI-driven chatbots enhances customer service and engagement without necessitating round-the-clock human oversight.

Streamlining Operations: Many tasks currently performed manually can be automated using various AI methodologies:
- **Process Automation**: Robotic Process Automation (RPA) and AI can automate routine tasks, freeing up staff for more complex work.
- **Supply Chain Optimization**: AI can help optimize supply chain logistics, from demand forecasting to inventory management, reducing costs and improving efficiency.

Security and Risk Management: The security domain has become increasingly complex. Relying solely on human vigilance is becoming more challenging.
- **Threat Detection and Response**: AI systems can identify and respond to cyber threats more rapidly than traditional methods.
- **Fraud Detection**: AI plays a significant role in analyzing transaction patterns to detect and prevent fraudulent activities.

Innovation and Product Development
- **Market Analysis**: Employing AI to analyze market trends and consumer feedback for product development provides valuable insights.
- **Design and Testing**: The latest AI trends demonstrate how it accelerates the design process, from conceptualization to prototype testing, through rapid simulations and data analysis.

For each of these areas, real-world examples and case studies are provided below.

Healthcare: IBM Watson Health

- **Use Case**: IBM Watson Health supports healthcare professionals in diagnosing and determining treatments. Watson analyzes the meaning and context of structured and unstructured data in clinical notes and reports, compares it with a vast medical literature database, and suggests potential treatment options for patients.

Retail: Stitch Fix
- **Use Case**: Stitch Fix, an online personal styling service, uses AI to personalize clothing selections for its customers. AI algorithms analyze customer preferences, feedback, and fashion trends to assist stylists in choosing the right items for individual customers, improving customer satisfaction and retention.

Finance: JPMorgan Chase's COIN
- **Use Case**: JPMorgan Chase employs a program named COIN (Contract Intelligence) to automate commercial loan agreement analysis and interpretation. This AI-driven system significantly reduces document review time from 360,000 hours annually to mere seconds per document, enhancing efficiency and accuracy.

Manufacturing: Siemens and General Electric (GE)
- **Use Case**: Siemens and GE utilize AI in their manufacturing processes to predict when machines will likely fail or require maintenance. This predictive maintenance approach, using AI algorithms to analyze sensor data on equipment, reduces downtime and saves costs.

E-commerce: Amazon
- **Use Case**: Amazon uses AI for various purposes, including personalized product recommendations, optimizing logistics and delivery routes, and managing inventory. Its AI algorithms analyze customer behavior, preferences, and purchasing history to enhance the shopping experience and operational efficiency.

Automotive: Tesla

- **Use Case**: Tesla's Autopilot system employs AI for semi-autonomous driving. It processes sensor and camera data to navigate roads, detect obstacles, and make real-time driving decisions, advancing self-driving vehicle development.

Entertainment: Netflix
- **Use Case**: Netflix utilizes AI to personalize content recommendations for its users. By analyzing viewing history, search queries, and user ratings, Netflix's AI algorithms can suggest shows and movies likely to appeal to individual users, enhancing engagement.

Customer Service: Zoho's Zia
- **Use Case**: Zia, Zoho's AI-powered assistant, improves customer service by analyzing customer interaction data to identify trends, sentiments, and anomalies. It also helps automate responses to common inquiries, enabling faster and more efficient customer support.

Some specific use cases in the Telecom industry are:
- **Network Optimization and Maintenance**: AI algorithms analyze network traffic in real-time to predict and prevent congestion, ensuring optimal network performance. Predictive maintenance uses AI to forecast equipment failures before they occur, minimizing downtime.
- **Security and Fraud Detection**: AI systems analyze call patterns and usage data to detect unusual behavior indicative of fraud, such as SIM box fraud or subscription fraud. This helps telecom companies minimize losses and protect their customers.
- **Predictive Analytics for Churn Reduction**: By analyzing customer behavior and usage patterns, AI can identify subscribers at risk of churning. Telecom companies can then proactively offer incentives, discounts, or personalized services to retain these customers.
- **Quality of Service (QoS) Management**: AI monitors network parameters in real-time to ensure that QoS

levels meet customer expectations and service level agreements (SLAs). It can dynamically adjust network resources to maintain high-quality voice and data services.

These examples illustrate AI's broad applicability and transformative potential across different sectors, showcasing how businesses can leverage AI to enhance efficiency, personalize services, and drive innovation.

Here are some practical steps for implementing AI technologies, including cooperation with partners and vendors:

- Invest in AI infrastructure and talent to effectively develop and deploy AI-driven solutions.
- Collaborate with technology partners and vendors who specialize in AI to access advanced capabilities.
- Continuously assess and adjust AI strategies to align with emerging technology trends and customer expectations.
- Maintain transparency and accountability in AI systems to preserve trust and ensure compliance with regulatory standards.
- Cultivate a culture of innovation and experimentation to discover new ways to utilize AI across various business areas.
- Regularly assess internal processes that can be automated or enhanced through AI technologies.

By engaging in these practical actions and continuous learning, you will gradually implement and utilize many of the latest technologies, along with the necessary tools and security measures to ensure their successful operation.

Key takeaways for the Chapter 10: Technologies Transforming the IT Landscape

Develop a Cloud Approach: To maximize flexibility and efficiency, adopt a cloud strategy applicable to your business. This approach ensures you're prepared to adapt to changing business needs and technological advancements.

Incorporate Green IT Practices in Procurement Policies: Make environmental sustainability a core criterion in your IT procurement process. By choosing energy-efficient hardware, opting for vendors with strong sustainability records, and investing in renewable energy sources for your data centers, you can significantly reduce your carbon footprint and operational costs.

Leverage AI for strategic advantage: Utilize AI-driven analytics to transform raw data into actionable insights. Implement AI tools to automate data analysis processes, enabling you to quickly identify trends, optimize operations, and make informed decisions. This not only boosts efficiency but also drives competitive advantage in an increasingly data-driven world.

Your records: I encourage you to write down your conclusion, ideas, and actions from this Chapter. This action will ensure that the information you get will have practical utilization.

CHAPTER 11. IT LEADER CHECKLIST (BONUS CHAPTER)

As I stated at the beginning of the book, my goal was to provide a comprehensive and practical guide for any IT Leader. I believe that the methodologies presented in this book will equip you to not just manage but also enhance your role, leading to the achievement of broader organizational goals.

Here, in this Chapter, I wanted to provide an additional tool, which can be referred to as the "**IT Leader Checklist**."

This tool can be useful for examining your position from various angles and across different domains, and to identify any additional responsibilities that might fall under your purview.

IT Leader / CIO Checklist

An IT Leader plays a crucial role in aligning the IT strategy with the organization's goals and ensuring the efficient operation of IT services. Here's a comprehensive checklist that an IT Leader might use to manage their responsibilities effectively:

Strategic Planning
☐ Define IT strategic goals aligned with business objectives.
☐ Develop an IT roadmap for technology adoption and digital transformation.
☐ Conduct a SWOT analysis to identify strengths, weaknesses, opportunities, and threats in the IT landscape.
☐ Ensure IT governance frameworks are in place and compliant with industry standards.

Budget Management
☐ Prepare the IT budget, including CAPEX and OPEX, ensuring alignment with strategic goals.
☐ Implement cost-control measures to optimize spending.
☐ Monitor and report on IT spending against the budget regularly.

Cybersecurity and Compliance
☐ Assess and strengthen the organization's cybersecurity posture.

☐ Ensure compliance with relevant data protection regulations (e.g., GDPR, HIPAA).
☐ Develop and test incident response and disaster recovery plans.

Technology Management

☐ Oversee the management of IT infrastructure, ensuring reliability and scalability.
☐ Evaluate and implement new technologies to drive innovation and efficiency.
☐ Manage software and hardware lifecycle, from procurement to disposal.

Project and Portfolio Management

☐ Prioritize IT projects based on business impact and resource availability.
☐ Monitor project progress, ensuring they are delivered on time, within scope, and budget.
☐ Implement project management best practices and methodologies (e.g., Agile, Waterfall).

Vendor and Stakeholder Management

☐ Negotiate and manage contracts with IT vendors and service providers.
☐ Build strong relationships with key stakeholders, including business leaders and external partners.
☐ Ensure IT services meet or exceed expectations through SLAs and performance metrics.

Team Leadership and Development

☐ Foster a culture of innovation, collaboration, and continuous improvement within the IT team.
☐ Develop talent through training, mentorship, and career progression opportunities.
☐ Recruit and retain skilled IT professionals to fill key positions.

Performance Monitoring

☐ Implement IT KPIs and dashboards to monitor and report on IT performance.

☐ Conduct regular IT reviews and audits to identify areas for improvement.

☐ Adjust IT strategies and operations based on performance data and feedback.

Risk Management

☐ Identify IT risks related to security, data privacy, and technology obsolescence.

☐ Implement risk mitigation strategies and regularly review risk assessments.

☐ Ensure business continuity through robust risk management practices.

Innovation and Digital Transformation

☐ Foster a culture that encourages innovation and experimentation.

☐ Lead digital transformation initiatives to improve customer experience and operational efficiency.

☐ Stay abreast of industry trends and emerging technologies that could impact the organization.

IT Service Management

☐ Ensure ITIL/ITSM (Information Technology Infrastructure Library / IT Service Management) processes are in place for effective IT service delivery.

☐ Monitor service desk performance to improve user satisfaction and reduce downtimes.

☐ Implement continuous service improvement processes to enhance IT service quality.

This checklist can help IT Leaders ensure they are covering the critical aspects of their role.

It should be adapted to fit the specific needs and context of your organization.

CONCLUSION

YOU ARE EQUIPPED FOR YOUR JOURNEY.

Navigating the role of a IT and Technology leader within a company is undeniably challenging. On the one hand, you must actively engage with the business's strategic challenges, while on the other, you are tasked with maintaining the seamless operation of all technology components and ensuring that your technology team is equipped to foster both growth and stability.

I believe this book serves as your guide through the complexities of IT Leadership and Technology Management.

All the real-life cases presented are genuine, with minor modifications made solely to eliminate any confidential elements. My primary objective was to share authentic examples from real-life situations without causing harm to anyone. Building a foundation rooted in practical experience is essential, and that is precisely what I aim to provide.

I invite you to share your thoughts, feedback, and requests for additional content. I am eager to enhance, modify, and furnish you with more practical information that will empower you to excel in your role effectively.

You can contact me here:

LinkedIn – https://www.linkedin.com/in/radu-spataru

X (twitter.com) - https://twitter.com/RaduSpataru3

Website – https://ingines.pro , https://spataruradu.gumroad.com

ABBREVIATIONS USED IN THIS BOOK.

Abbreviation	Full-Form/Description
CIO	The Chief Information Officer (CIO) holds a pivotal role in managing an organization's information technology strategy and infrastructure. This position is akin to roles such as IT Director or Head of IT.
CTO	Chief Technical Officer or Chief Technology Officer (CTO) is a leadership position responsible for overseeing the technological aspects of a company. While in some companies, the role may be like CIO, in specific domains like Telecom or Development-oriented companies, distinctions exist.
SMART	SMART is a method employed to articulate Objectives and Key Performance Indicators (KPIs) with clarity. The acronym stands for Specific, Measurable, Achievable, Relevant, and Time-bound. This methodology ensures that goals are well-defined, quantifiable, realistic, aligned with broader objectives, and have specific timeframes for

	accomplishment.
SLA	Service Level Agreement (SLA) is a contractual arrangement between a service provider and a customer. It outlines the expected level of service, including quality, availability, and the responsibilities of each party. SLAs are commonly utilized in various industries, including information technology, telecommunications, and business process outsourcing.
CAPEX	Capital Expenditure (CAPEX) refers to the funds a company invests in acquiring, upgrading, or maintaining physical assets. These investments are made with the expectation of generating future benefits for the organization. CAPEX is distinct from Operational Expenditure (OPEX) as it involves long-term asset-related investments.
OPEX	Operational Expenditure (OPEX) encompasses the ongoing costs incurred by a business in its day-to-day operations to sustain its essential functions. These expenses include utilities, rent, salaries, maintenance, and other operational costs. In contrast to CAPEX, which involves long-term investments, OPEX is associated with regular, short-term costs crucial for daily business activities.
RFP	Request for Proposal (RFP) is a formal document created by an organization to

	solicit bids or proposals from qualified vendors or service providers for a specific project or service. The RFP outlines project requirements, scope of work, expected deliverables, and relevant details, providing a structured approach for organizations to communicate their needs and evaluate detailed proposals from potential suppliers.
RFI	An RFI (request for information) is a formal process for gathering information from potential suppliers of a good or service.
SPOC	Single point of contact - key person responsible for a domain and/or project. If this person is responsible for a project inside IT, she or he can easily get the status, escalate, and/or help the internal team excel in this project
PMO	Project Management Office - team or position of person(s) responsible for the project management process inside the company.
GDPR	The General Data Protection Regulation (GDPR) is a comprehensive data protection law that became enforceable on May 25, 2018, in the European Union (EU). It sets guidelines for the collection, processing, and storage of personal information of individuals within the EU and the European Economic Area (EEA). The GDPR aims to give individuals more control over their personal data and to harmonize data privacy laws across Europe.
HIPAA	The Health Insurance Portability and Accountability Act (HIPAA) is a US law enacted in 1996, designed to protect the privacy and security of individuals'

	medical information and ensure health insurance coverage for workers and their families when they change or lose their jobs. HIPAA establishes national standards for electronic healthcare transactions, healthcare providers, health plans, and other entities that process health information.
E2E	End to End approach
DR	Disaster Recovery (DR) in the IT domain refers to a set of policies, tools, and procedures that enable the recovery or continuation of vital technology infrastructure and systems following a natural or human-induced disaster.
BC	Business Continuity (BC) refers to the processes, policies, and procedures that enable an organization to maintain essential functions or quickly resume them in the event of a major disruption, whether due to natural disasters, cyber-attacks, or other significant threats.
ITIL	Information Technology Infrastructure Library: ITIL is a set of detailed practices for IT service management (ITSM) that focuses on aligning IT services with the needs of business. It provides a practical framework for identifying, planning, delivering, and supporting IT services to the business.
ITSM	IT Service Management: ITSM refers to the entirety of activities, policies, and processes that organizations use to design, deliver, manage, and improve the IT services provided to customers. It's oriented towards the effective and efficient delivery of IT services to support business objectives.
CMDB	Configuration Management Database - A CMDB provides a common place to

	store data associated with IT assets and configuration items.
SWOT	SWOT analysis (or SWOT matrix) is a strategic planning and strategic management technique used to help a person or organization identify Strengths, Weaknesses, Opportunities, and Threats related to business competition or project planning.

LIST OF DIAGRAMS AND TABLES

Picture 1: We are busy ... to do the transformation. (Chapter 1)

Picture 2. Backup and Handover process. (Chapter "C")

Picture 3. Example of Business and IT strategy on one slide. (Chapter 3, point 3.5)

Picture 4. Example IT Strategy Execution Roadmap on 2 slides. (Chapter 4)

Picture 5. Diagram of Waterfall methodology (Chapter 9, point 9.1)

Picture 6. Diagram of Agile methodology. (Chapter 9, point 9.2)

Table 1. IT assessment template (Chapter 2)

Table 2. Example of Information Categorization. (Chapter 5, point 5.2)

Table 3. Core differences between Business Continuity and Disaster Recovery. (Chapter 5, point 5.7)

Table 4. Salary Grid Example. (Chapter 6, point 6.3)

Table 5. Example of SWOT analysis - select the IT tool X (Chapter 7, point 7.3)

Table 6. Example of IT KPIs. (Chapter 7, point 7.7)

Table 7. IT Budget - CAPEX. (Chapter 8, point 8.3)

Table 8. IT Budget - OPEX. (Chapter 8, point 8.3)

Table 9. General guide for PM methodology usage. (Chapter 9, point 9.3)

REFERENCES

Quotes used in the Book.

1. "Today's IT leaders need to be business leaders first, with a strong understanding of the organization's strategic goals, market context, and business processes." Jill Dyche - from the book "The New IT: How Technology Leaders are Enabling Business Strategy in the Digital Age" by the same author, is a book that discusses the evolving role of IT in organization.

2. "Productivity is meaningless unless you know what your goal is." by Eliyahu M. Goldratt and Jeff Cox – from the Book "The Goal: A Process of Ongoing Improvement" by Eliyahu M. Goldratt and Jeff Cox is a seminal work in the field of operations management and business efficiency.

3. "Ideas are easy. Execution is everything." by John Doerr – from the Book "Measure What Matters" by John Doerr is a book that emphasizes the importance of goal-setting and focus in organizations.

4. "The CIO Paradox is a set of contradictions that lies at the core of IT leadership. The paradox encapsulates the daily challenges that CIOs face, and it is what makes the role so difficult, and so interesting." by Martha Heller – from the Book "The CIO Paradox: Battling the Contradictions of IT Leadership" by Martha Heller provides valuable insights into the challenges and paradoxes faced by Chief Information Officers (CIOs) in the rapidly evolving field of information technology.

6. "Approximately 75% of venture-backed startups fail. The number is difficult to pin down, and some estimates suggest it could be even higher." Elizabeth Pollman, University of Pennsylvania, in the study about reasons of Startup Failure.

ABOUT THE AUTHOR

Radu Spataru

After spending numerous years as an IT expert in various domains, my professional journey has been characterized by continual growth and a steadfast commitment to driving positive change.

As I advanced from being an expert to taking on management roles, including Team Leader, IT Manager, Project Manager, and eventually CIO/CTO/CEO, each new position offered not only better salary and conditions but also a host of challenges. This transition required a significant shift in my thinking; I realized that I couldn't tackle tasks in the same manner as before, even with my superior understanding of the work and processes. New management responsibilities surfaced, encompassing budgeting, team leadership, conflict resolution, and more.

With nearly two decades of experience in Technology Management, I became inspired to distill the valuable insights I had acquired over the years into clear and concise guides, aiming to share them with others.

www.ingramcontent.com/pod-product-compliance
Lightning Source LLC
Chambersburg PA
CBHW052145220526
45471CB00004B/1537

Prospecção sem medo: como conquistar clientes quando você mais precisa

Copyright © 2024 Reginaldo Osnildo
Todos os direitos reservados.

APRESENTAÇÃO

INTRODUÇÃO À PROSPECÇÃO ATIVA

MUDANDO A MENTALIDADE SOBRE VENDAS

IDENTIFICAÇÃO DO PÚBLICO-ALVO

CONSTRUINDO SUA CONFIANÇA EM VENDAS

DESENVOLVENDO UMA PROPOSTA DE VALOR IRRESISTÍVEL

TÉCNICAS DE COMUNICAÇÃO EFICAZES

O PODER DO NETWORKING

CRIANDO UM PLANO DE PROSPECÇÃO PERSONALIZADO

CHAMADA FRIA COM CONFIANÇA

ESTRATÉGIAS DE ENVIOS DE E-MAILS FRIOS QUE FUNCIONAM

UTILIZANDO AS REDES SOCIAIS PARA PROSPECÇÃO

GESTÃO DO TEMPO PARA PROSPECÇÃO

RESPONDENDO A OBJEÇÕES

SEGUINDO SEM SER INVASIVO

USANDO CONTEÚDO PARA ATRAIR CLIENTES

ESTRATÉGIAS DE SEO PARA GERAÇÃO DE LEADS

FERRAMENTAS DIGITAIS E AUTOMAÇÃO EM PROSPECÇÃO

CRIANDO E MANTENDO RELACIONAMENTOS DURADOUROS COM CLIENTES

MEDINDO O SUCESSO DA SUA PROSPECÇÃO

MANEIRAS CRIATIVAS PARA GERAR LEADS

VENDENDO SEM VENDER

NEGOCIAÇÃO E FECHAMENTO DE VENDAS

AUTOCUIDADO E GESTÃO DO ESTRESSE EM VENDAS

PLANO DE AÇÃO DE 30 DIAS PARA PROSPECÇÃO ATIVA

REGINALDO OSNILDO

APRESENTAÇÃO

Bem-vindo a uma jornada transformadora que promete redefinir sua relação com a prospecção ativa e com as vendas. Se você está lendo estas palavras, é provável que esteja em busca de algo que possa virar o jogo a seu favor, algo que transforme dificuldades em oportunidades e medo em motivação. Este não é apenas mais um livro sobre vendas; é um convite para você adentrar em um caminho menos percorrido, onde a prospecção se torna a sua maior aliada na busca pelo sucesso.

Seja você um empreendedor individual ou o coração de uma pequena empresa, enfrentar o desafio da prospecção ativa pode parecer uma montanha íngreme demais para escalar. A boa notícia? Você não está sozinho. Este livro, **Prospecção sem medo: como conquistar clientes quando você mais precisa**, é projetado com você em mente, trazendo não apenas um compêndio de técnicas práticas e estratégias testadas, mas também uma nova perspectiva sobre como encarar e superar as barreiras que se interpõem entre você e o seu crescimento.

Através das páginas a seguir, vou guiá-lo por uma transformação profunda, atualizando conceitos tradicionais de prospecção para o nosso tempo, simplificando processos e, o mais importante, ajudando a construir um mindset que transformará o medo de vender em entusiasmo para conectar, engajar e, finalmente, conquistar.

Cada capítulo deste livro foi cuidadosamente desenhado para se complementar, formando um mapa que o levará desde os fundamentos da prospecção ativa até as estratégias mais avançadas de manutenção de relacionamentos duradouros com seus clientes. Você aprenderá a identificar seu público-alvo, desenvolver uma proposta de valor irresistível, utilizar as redes sociais a seu favor, gerenciar seu tempo de prospecção eficazmente, e muito mais.

Este não é apenas um livro; é uma experiência de aprendizado interativa que se propõe a ser um ponto de virada em sua carreira e em sua vida. Ao longo de sua leitura, você encontrará convites para refletir sobre suas próprias práticas e desafios para tirá-lo da zona de conforto que mostrarão o poder real da persistência, da inovação e da resiliência.

Portanto, convido você a virar a página e começar esta viagem comigo. Prepare-se para desbloquear o potencial da prospecção ativa, transformando-a de uma fonte de estresse em um motor potente para alimentar suas ambições, sustentar sua família e crescer seu negócio. A cada capítulo, um novo horizonte se abrirá, e juntos, passo a passo, construiremos uma ponte sobre qualquer abismo de dúvida ou medo, rumo ao sucesso que você merece e pode definitivamente alcançar.

Avance para o próximo capítulo, onde mergulhamos fundo na **INTRODUÇÃO À PROSPECÇÃO ATIVA**, compreendendo a essencialidade dessa habilidade em sua jornada para o crescimento sustentável do negócio. Prepare-se para desvendar o primeiro passo em direção a uma prospecção sem medo.

Atenciosamente

Prof. Dr. Reginaldo Osnildo

INTRODUÇÃO À PROSPECÇÃO ATIVA

A prospecção ativa é o coração pulsante de qualquer negócio que busca não apenas sobreviver, mas prosperar em um mercado cada vez mais competitivo. Neste capítulo, vamos desvendar a essencialidade da prospecção ativa, entendendo como ela pode se tornar a espinha dorsal para sustentar e ampliar sua base de clientes, e por consequência, seu negócio.

A FUNDAÇÃO DO SUCESSO EMPRESARIAL

No mundo dos negócios, a capacidade de gerar novos leads e converter esses leads em clientes pagantes é o que separa as empresas de sucesso daquelas que lutam para manter as luzes acesas. A prospecção ativa, nesse sentido, é muito mais do que uma tática de vendas; é uma filosofia empresarial que coloca o crescimento sustentável no centro de todas as atividades comerciais.

POR QUE A PROSPECÇÃO ATIVA?

Você pode se perguntar: por que focar em prospecção ativa quando existem tantas outras estratégias de marketing e vendas disponíveis? A resposta é simples: controle e iniciativa. Ao dominar a arte da prospecção ativa, você assume o controle do seu fluxo de vendas. Você não fica à mercê de campanhas de marketing passivas, esperando que potenciais clientes o encontrem. Em vez disso, você toma a iniciativa, buscando ativamente por aqueles que se beneficiarão mais do que você tem a oferecer.

DESMISTIFICANDO A PROSPECÇÃO

Muitos empreendedores e vendedores veem a prospecção como uma tarefa árdua e muitas vezes intimidadora. Isso geralmente se deve a uma mistura de medo de rejeição, falta de confiança nas próprias habilidades de vendas e uma compreensão equivocada do que realmente significa prospectar. Neste livro, vamos desmistificar essas percepções, mostrando que a prospecção pode ser uma atividade empolgante, gratificante e incrivelmente eficaz quando feita corretamente.

O PAPEL DA TECNOLOGIA NA PROSPECÇÃO MODERNA

No ambiente de vendas de hoje, a tecnologia desempenha um papel crucial na prospecção ativa. Ferramentas digitais e plataformas de automação não apenas tornam o processo mais eficiente, mas também permitem uma personalização e segmentação sem precedentes. Isso significa que você pode alcançar o público certo, com a mensagem certa, no momento certo, aumentando significativamente suas chances de sucesso.

CONSTRUINDO RELACIONAMENTOS, NÃO APENAS FAZENDO VENDAS

Um equívoco comum sobre a prospecção ativa é que ela se concentra exclusivamente em fazer uma venda. No entanto, a verdadeira essência da prospecção é construir relacionamentos. Cada interação é uma oportunidade para entender melhor as necessidades, desejos e desafios do seu público-alvo, permitindo que você ofereça soluções que realmente façam a diferença em suas vidas ou negócios.

PREPARANDO-SE PARA A JORNADA

Conforme você avança neste capítulo, o convido a abordar a prospecção ativa não como uma tarefa, mas como uma jornada de descoberta. Vamos explorar técnicas, estratégias e mentalidades que não apenas facilitarão esse processo, mas também o tornarão mais eficaz e gratificante.

Ao fechar este capítulo, espero que você esteja não apenas mais informado sobre a importância crítica da prospecção ativa, mas também inspirado a abraçá-la como uma ferramenta poderosa para o crescimento. E com essa base sólida, estamos prontos para mergulhar ainda mais fundo, transformando a percepção sobre vendas de uma tarefa intimidadora para uma atividade empolgante no próximo capítulo, **MUDANDO A MENTALIDADE SOBRE VENDAS**. Prepare-se para transformar seu mindset e abrir as portas para o sucesso em vendas como você nunca viu antes.

MUDANDO A MENTALIDADE SOBRE VENDAS

Vender é uma arte, um estudo de conexão humana, comunicação e psicologia. Mas, por que tantos de nós tremem só de pensar em "fazer uma venda"? Este capítulo é um convite para você repensar e transformar sua percepção sobre vendas, de uma tarefa intimidadora para uma jornada empolgante de crescimento pessoal e sucesso empresarial.

VENDAS: O MONSTRO SOB A CAMA

Para muitos, a venda é o monstro sob a cama. É aquela atividade temida que evocamos em nossas mentes como algo a ser evitado a todo custo. Esse medo geralmente é alimentado por preconceitos sobre vendas serem manipulativas, forçadas ou invasivas. A verdade? Vendas, em sua essência, são sobre criar valor e resolver problemas.

A MENTALIDADE DE SERVIÇO

A chave para transformar sua percepção sobre vendas começa com a mentalidade de serviço. Quando você muda o foco de "eu preciso vender" para "eu tenho algo valioso que pode ajudar alguém", você começa a ver vendas sob uma nova luz. Vender se torna menos sobre persuadir e mais sobre escutar, entender e responder às necessidades de seus clientes.

APRENDER A AMAR O PROCESSO

Amar o processo de vendas pode parecer uma tarefa hercúlea no início, mas é absolutamente possível. Comece celebrando pequenas vitórias e aprendizados, independentemente do resultado. Cada "não" é uma oportunidade para refinar sua abordagem, cada feedback é um presente para melhorar. Quando você se concentra no processo, e não apenas no resultado, a jornada de vendas se torna mais gratificante.

CONSTRUINDO CONFIANÇA, DENTRO E FORA

A confiança é o alicerce de qualquer relacionamento de venda bem-sucedido. Mas para construir confiança com seus clientes, você primeiro precisa confiar em si mesmo e no valor que está oferecendo. Isso começa com um profundo conhecimento do seu produto ou serviço e uma crença sincera em seu potencial para fazer a diferença.

ENCARANDO O MEDO DE FRENTE

O medo da rejeição é, sem dúvida, um dos maiores obstáculos na venda. No entanto, encarar esse medo de frente é crucial para transformar sua mentalidade sobre vendas. Entenda que a rejeição não é pessoal; é apenas uma parte do processo. A cada "não" que você recebe, você está um passo mais perto de um "sim".

A VENDA COMO UMA JORNADA DE DESCOBERTA

Vendas devem ser vistas como uma jornada de descoberta, tanto para você quanto para o seu cliente. Através do processo de vendas, você tem a oportunidade de descobrir as necessidades ocultas de seus clientes, proporcionando-lhes soluções que nem sabiam que precisavam. Isso transforma vendas de uma tarefa em uma missão.

Agora que começamos a transformar sua percepção sobre vendas, o próximo passo é identificar e compreender profundamente o seu público-alvo. No próximo capítulo, **IDENTIFICAÇÃO DO PÚBLICO-ALVO**, vamos mergulhar nas técnicas e estratégias para encontrar e entender seu mercado ideal. Preparado para descobrir onde suas ofertas ressoarão mais fortemente e criar conexões autênticas que convertam? Avance para o próximo capítulo, onde sua jornada de transformação continua.

IDENTIFICAÇÃO DO PÚBLICO-ALVO

Conhecer profundamente quem são seus clientes potenciais é a pedra angular de qualquer estratégia de vendas eficaz. Este capítulo é dedicado a desvendar os métodos para encontrar e compreender seu público-alvo, garantindo que suas ofertas não só sejam ouvidas mas ressoem de forma significativa com quem mais importa: seus futuros clientes.

O QUE É PÚBLICO-ALVO?

Público-alvo refere-se ao grupo específico de pessoas ou empresas que têm maior probabilidade de se beneficiar de seus produtos ou serviços. Identificar seu público-alvo não é apenas saber quem eles são, mas entender suas necessidades, desejos, dores e como sua oferta se encaixa na vida ou no negócio deles.

A IMPORTÂNCIA DE CONHECER SEU PÚBLICO

Conhecer seu público-alvo não é uma tarefa acadêmica; é um imperativo estratégico. Quando você tem clareza sobre com quem está falando, suas mensagens de marketing e vendas se tornam mais direcionadas, pessoais e eficazes. Isso não apenas aumenta suas chances de conversão, mas também constrói uma base de clientes mais engajada e fiel.

COMEÇANDO COM PESQUISA DE MERCADO

A jornada para identificar seu público-alvo começa com a pesquisa de mercado. Utilize ferramentas online, pesquisas, entrevistas e dados de mercado existentes para coletar informações sobre as características demográficas, comportamentais e psicográficas de seus clientes potenciais. Essas informações formarão a base para suas personas de cliente, representações semifictícias de seu cliente ideal.

CRIANDO PERSONAS DE CLIENTE

As personas de cliente são ferramentas incrivelmente úteis para visualizar e compreender seu público-alvo. Elas ajudam a humanizar dados demográficos e psicográficos, transformando-os em personagens relacionáveis com os quais você e sua equipe podem se identificar. Ao desenvolver suas personas, inclua não apenas informações demográficas, mas também suas motivações, desafios e como eles interagem com sua marca ou setor.

APROFUNDANDO-SE NAS NECESSIDADES DO SEU PÚBLICO

Entender seu público-alvo requer mais do que apenas conhecer suas características básicas; exige aprofundar-se em suas necessidades específicas e como seu produto ou serviço pode atender a essas necessidades. Isso significa escutar ativamente, seja através de feedback direto, análise de comportamento online ou estudos de mercado. Quanto mais você souber sobre o que seu público precisa e valoriza, mais eficaz será sua capacidade de se conectar com eles.

UTILIZANDO FEEDBACK PARA REFINAR SEU FOCO

O processo de identificação do público-alvo não é estático; é um ciclo contínuo de aprendizado e ajuste. Use o feedback de seus clientes existentes para refinar suas personas de cliente e estratégias de abordagem. Este feedback é um tesouro de insights que podem ajudá-lo a ajustar sua oferta e mensagens de forma que ressoe ainda mais profundamente com seu público.

Com um entendimento claro de seu público-alvo, você está agora equipado para mover-se adiante com confiança. Suas estratégias de marketing e vendas podem ser mais focadas, personalizadas e eficazes, construindo a base para um negócio sustentável e em crescimento.

No próximo capítulo, **CONSTRUINDO SUA CONFIANÇA EM VENDAS**, vamos explorar como você pode fortalecer sua autoconfiança e apresentar suas ofertas com convicção, garantindo que seu público não apenas ouça, mas responda. Prepare-se para mergulhar profundamente em si mesmo, descobrindo e desbloqueando o vendedor confiante que você nasceu para ser.

CONSTRUINDO SUA CONFIANÇA EM VENDAS

A confiança é a moeda mais valiosa no reino das vendas. Não apenas a confiança em seu produto ou serviço, mas, mais crucialmente, a confiança em si mesmo como vendedor. Este capítulo é dedicado a fortalecer sua autoconfiança, capacitando-o a apresentar suas ofertas com convicção e autenticidade. Aqui, você aprenderá estratégias para construir e exibir uma confiança inabalável que atrairá clientes e fechará vendas.

A AUTOCONFIANÇA E SUAS RAÍZES

A autoconfiança em vendas começa com duas crenças fundamentais: acreditar no valor do que você oferece e acreditar em sua capacidade de comunicar esse valor. Isso significa conhecer seu produto ou serviço intimamente e reconhecer o impacto positivo que ele pode ter na vida dos seus clientes. Quando você opera a partir desse lugar de certeza, sua confiança naturalmente se eleva.

CONHECIMENTO É PODER

Uma das maneiras mais eficazes de construir confiança é através do aprofundamento no conhecimento sobre seu produto ou serviço. Quanto mais você souber, mais preparado você estará para responder a perguntas, resolver preocupações e destacar benefícios de maneira convincente. Dedique tempo para aprender não apenas as características do seu produto, mas também as histórias de sucesso de clientes, estudos de caso e os diferentes cenários de uso.

PRÁTICA LEVA À PERFEIÇÃO

A confiança também vem da prática. Isso significa praticar suas técnicas de vendas, seu discurso de vendas e suas respostas para objeções comuns. Quanto mais você praticar, especialmente em um ambiente de baixo risco, como role playing com um colega ou mentor, mais natural e confiante você se tornará em situações de vendas reais.

CELEBRANDO PEQUENAS VITÓRIAS

Cada pequena vitória é um degrau no caminho para construir sua confiança. Celebre cada venda, claro, mas também celebre os passos que levam a ela: uma boa conversa com um prospect, um feedback positivo, ou mesmo um "não" que teve um aprendizado valioso. Cada uma dessas experiências é um tijolo na construção da sua confiança.

LIDANDO COM A REJEIÇÃO

A rejeição é parte do processo de vendas, mas não precisa ser um golpe na sua confiança. Veja cada rejeição como uma oportunidade para aprender e crescer. Pergunte-se: O que posso aprender com isso? Há feedback que posso usar para melhorar? Ressignifique a rejeição como um passo necessário no caminho para o sucesso.

CONSTRUINDO RELACIONAMENTOS, NÃO APENAS VENDAS

Lembre-se de que vendas é, em sua essência, sobre construir relacionamentos. Quando você foca em entender e atender às necessidades dos seus clientes, em vez de simplesmente fechar uma venda, você cria conexões genuínas. Isso não só aumenta suas chances de sucesso, mas também fortalece sua confiança ao saber que você está fazendo a diferença.

A CONFIANÇA VEM DE DENTRO

Finalmente, trabalhe em sua autoconfiança fora do contexto de vendas. Isso pode incluir técnicas de mindfulness, exercícios de afirmação ou simplesmente dedicar tempo para atividades que o façam se sentir bem consigo mesmo. Quando você se sente confiante em sua vida pessoal, essa confiança se transpõe para sua vida profissional.

Com sua autoconfiança fortalecida, você está pronto para levar suas habilidades de vendas para o próximo nível. No próximo capítulo, **DESENVOLVENDO UMA PROPOSTA DE VALOR IRRESISTÍVEL**, vamos explorar como comunicar o valor do que você oferece de uma maneira que naturalmente atraia clientes para você. Prepare-se para aprender a arte de criar e apresentar propostas que fazem os clientes dizerem "sim".

DESENVOLVENDO UMA PROPOSTA DE VALOR IRRESISTÍVEL

No coração de cada transação de sucesso está uma proposta de valor clara, convincente e irresistível. Este capítulo é dedicado a ajudá-lo a desenvolver uma proposta de valor que se destaque, comunicando eficazmente o valor único que seu produto ou serviço oferece. Uma proposta de valor irresistível não só atrai clientes, mas também os convence de que o que você oferece é exatamente o que eles precisam.

ENTENDENDO PROPOSTA DE VALOR

Uma proposta de valor é uma promessa clara do benefício que se espera entregar aos seus clientes. É a razão pela qual um cliente deve escolher seu produto ou serviço em detrimento dos seus concorrentes. Ela deve ser simples, direta e focada nos benefícios reais que o cliente experimentará ao fazer a compra.

IDENTIFICANDO O VALOR CENTRAL

O primeiro passo para desenvolver uma proposta de valor irresistível é identificar o valor central do seu produto ou serviço. Pergunte a si mesmo: Qual problema meu produto/serviço resolve? Como ele melhora a vida ou o negócio dos meus clientes? Que necessidades específicas ele atende? O valor central deve ser algo que seu público-alvo verdadeiramente deseja ou precisa, algo que tenha um impacto significativo para eles.

FALE A LINGUAGEM DO SEU CLIENTE

Para que sua proposta de valor ressoe com seu público-alvo, é crucial comunicá-la na linguagem deles. Isso significa usar palavras e frases que eles entendem e que refletem seus desejos, necessidades e dores. Evite jargões técnicos ou linguagem corporativa genérica; seja específico, seja pessoal e seja relevante.

DIFERENCIE-SE DA CONCORRÊNCIA

Um dos componentes chave de uma proposta de valor irresistível é a diferenciação. O que faz seu produto ou serviço ser diferente – e melhor – do que o que está disponível no mercado? Concentre-se em seus pontos únicos de venda e destaque-os de forma clara. Seja específico sobre o que você oferece que ninguém mais pode.

DEMONSTRE O VALOR

Não basta apenas afirmar seu valor; você precisa demonstrá-lo. Isso pode ser feito através de estudos de caso, depoimentos, dados de performance ou qualquer outra evidência que comprove os benefícios do seu produto ou serviço. As pessoas tendem a acreditar no que veem, portanto, fornecer prova concreta do seu valor é essencial.

SIMPLIFIQUE SUA MENSAGEM

Uma proposta de valor eficaz é simples e direta ao ponto. Evite a tentação de incluir todos os recursos ou benefícios do seu produto ou serviço. Concentre-se no que é mais importante para seus clientes e apresente-o de forma clara e concisa. Uma mensagem simples tem mais chances de ser lembrada e compreendida.

TESTE E REFINE

Desenvolver uma proposta de valor é um processo iterativo. Teste diferentes versões com seu público-alvo para ver o que ressoa melhor. Peça feedback e esteja aberto para ajustar sua proposta com base no que você aprende. Uma proposta de valor pode sempre ser melhorada, então veja esse processo como uma jornada, não um destino.

Com uma proposta de valor irresistível em mãos, você está bem posicionado para capturar a atenção e o interesse de seus clientes potenciais. No próximo capítulo, **TÉCNICAS DE COMUNICAÇÃO EFICAZES**, vamos aprofundar em como você pode melhorar suas habilidades de comunicação para engajar e converter esses clientes potenciais de forma positiva. Esteja pronto para aprender a arte de comunicar-se de maneira que construa relacionamentos, gere confiança e impulsione vendas.

TÉCNICAS DE COMUNICAÇÃO EFICAZES

Comunicar-se de maneira eficaz é fundamental para engajar potenciais clientes e conduzi-los através do funil de vendas. Este capítulo se concentra em aprimorar suas habilidades de comunicação, capacitando-o a conectar-se autenticamente com seu público e a apresentar sua proposta de valor de forma convincente. Dominar a arte da comunicação não apenas fortalece suas vendas, mas também constrói relacionamentos duradouros com seus clientes.

COMPREENDENDO A COMUNICAÇÃO

A comunicação vai além das palavras que você escolhe; é sobre criar uma conexão. Para isso, é essencial entender não apenas o que você está comunicando, mas também como sua mensagem é recebida. Isso envolve não apenas a linguagem verbal, mas também a não verbal, como sua postura, gestos e expressão facial, bem como a habilidade de escutar ativamente.

ESCUTA ATIVA

Escutar ativamente é uma das habilidades mais subestimadas em vendas. Isso significa ouvir com a intenção de entender, não apenas para responder. Ao praticar a escuta ativa, você não só demonstra respeito pelo seu interlocutor, mas também ganha insights valiosos sobre suas necessidades e preocupações, o que pode ajudá-lo a moldar sua comunicação de forma mais eficaz.

AJUSTE SUA MENSAGEM

Uma técnica de comunicação eficaz é a capacidade de ajustar sua mensagem com base no seu público. Isso pode envolver modificar o nível de complexidade da sua linguagem, mudar o foco da sua mensagem para alinhar melhor com as necessidades do ouvinte, ou até adaptar seu estilo de comunicação para combinar com o do seu cliente. A flexibilidade na comunicação mostra empatia e aumenta sua capacidade de conectar.

CLAREZA E CONCISÃO

Na comunicação, menos é mais. Mensagens claras e concisas são mais facilmente compreendidas e lembradas. Evite o excesso de jargões técnicos e não sobrecarregue seu cliente com informações desnecessárias. Concentre-se em comunicar sua proposta de valor de forma direta, destacando os benefícios mais relevantes para o cliente.

O PODER DA NARRATIVA

Histórias têm o poder de capturar a atenção e conectar em um nível emocional. Ao incorporar narrativas – seja contando casos de sucesso de clientes ou compartilhando uma experiência pessoal – você pode tornar sua mensagem mais relacionável e memorável. As histórias também são uma excelente maneira de demonstrar o valor do seu produto ou serviço de forma tangível.

COMUNICAÇÃO NÃO VERBAL

A comunicação não verbal, como contato visual, gestos e tom de voz, desempenha um papel crucial em como sua mensagem é recebida. Estes elementos podem reforçar sua mensagem, transmitir confiança e ajudar a estabelecer uma conexão mais forte. Esteja consciente de sua linguagem corporal e assegure-se de que ela esteja alinhada com o que você está dizendo.

FEEDBACK COMO FERRAMENTA

Veja o feedback não como crítica, mas como uma oportunidade valiosa de aprendizado e aprimoramento. Peça feedback regularmente e use-o para refinar suas habilidades de comunicação. Esteja aberto a ajustar seu estilo com base nas respostas que você recebe para melhor atender às necessidades de seu público.

Dominar a comunicação eficaz é um passo essencial para se tornar um vendedor de sucesso. No próximo capítulo, **O PODER DO NETWORKING**, vamos explorar como você pode utilizar sua rede existente para abrir portas e gerar leads. Prepare-se para aprender estratégias para expandir sua rede de forma significativa e como usar essas conexões para impulsionar seu sucesso em vendas.

O PODER DO NETWORKING

Networking não é apenas uma técnica de desenvolvimento de negócios; é uma arte que, quando bem executada, pode abrir portas inimagináveis, gerar leads valiosos e estabelecer parcerias duradouras. Este capítulo mergulha nas estratégias eficazes de networking, ajudando você a utilizar sua rede existente e expandi-la de maneira que suporte e acelere seus esforços de prospecção.

ENTENDENDO O NETWORKING

Networking vai além de coletar cartões de visita; é sobre construir relações genuínas e de confiança. Cada pessoa que você conhece tem potencial para se tornar um cliente, um parceiro, ou até mesmo um promotor do seu negócio. A chave é abordar o networking com a mentalidade correta, focando em como você pode agregar valor aos outros, em vez de apenas o que você pode ganhar.

COMECE COM SUA REDE EXISTENTE

Sua rede atual é o ponto de partida perfeito. Considere familiares, amigos, colegas de trabalho anteriores, clientes e até mesmo conhecidos casuais. Faça um inventário das pessoas que você já conhece e identifique como elas podem se encaixar em sua estratégia de networking. Uma conexão pessoal pré-existente pode ser um caminho poderoso para introduções e recomendações.

ESTRATÉGIAS PARA EXPANDIR SUA REDE

- **Eventos de networking:** Participar de eventos específicos do setor ou de networking local é uma maneira excelente de conhecer novas pessoas. Vá preparado com uma introdução breve e memorável sobre você e seu negócio.

- **Grupos e associações profissionais:** Junte-se a grupos relevantes ao seu setor, tanto online quanto offline. Esses são ótimos lugares para encontrar pessoas com interesses e desafios similares.

- **Plataformas de mídia social:** LinkedIn, Twitter e grupos específicos do setor no Facebook podem ser ferramentas poderosas para se conectar com profissionais da sua área. Compartilhe conteúdo valioso e envolva-se em conversas para aumentar sua visibilidade.

- **Voluntariado:** Oferecer seu tempo ou habilidades para causas ou organizações pode ser uma maneira não só de contribuir para sua comunidade, mas também de conhecer pessoas com valores semelhantes.

CONSTRUINDO RELACIONAMENTOS DE LONGO PRAZO

Networking eficaz é sobre nutrir relacionamentos, não apenas sobre fazer contato inicial. Mantenha-se em contato com sua rede através de mensagens regulares, compartilhando artigos de interesse, ou mesmo marcando encontros casuais. Lembre-se de que a reciprocidade é fundamental; procure maneiras de ajudar ou agregar valor aos outros sempre que possível.

NETWORKING DIGITAL

Em um mundo cada vez mais digital, sua presença online é tão importante quanto sua presença física. Mantenha seus perfis nas redes sociais atualizados e profissionais. Use essas plataformas para destacar seu conhecimento, compartilhar sucessos e contribuir para discussões relevantes. Além disso, considere criar conteúdo próprio para aumentar sua autoridade e visibilidade no setor.

A ETIQUETA DO NETWORKING

- **Seja autêntico:** As pessoas são atraídas por autenticidade. Seja você mesmo e mostre genuíno interesse pelos outros.

- **Escute mais do que fale:** Ouvir atentamente demonstra respeito e permite que você entenda melhor as necessidades e interesses da outra pessoa.

- **Siga através:** Se você prometeu enviar informações, fazer uma introdução ou compartilhar recursos, certifique-se de cumprir. Isso constrói confiança e credibilidade.

Com essas estratégias de networking em mãos, você está bem equipado para construir e cultivar uma rede de contatos que não apenas apoia seus objetivos de prospecção ativa, mas também enriquece sua jornada empresarial de maneiras que você talvez nem imagine. No próximo capítulo, **CRIANDO UM PLANO DE PROSPECÇÃO PERSONALIZADO**, vamos mergulhar nas táticas para criar um plano de ação sob medida que alavanque seus pontos fortes e maximize seus esforços de prospecção. Prepare-se para transformar seu networking em resultados concretos.

CRIANDO UM PLANO DE PROSPECÇÃO PERSONALIZADO

Após estabelecer uma base sólida de conhecimento sobre seu público-alvo, construir sua confiança em vendas, desenvolver uma proposta de valor irresistível, aprimorar suas técnicas de comunicação e expandir sua rede, o próximo passo é criar um plano de prospecção personalizado. Este capítulo irá orientá-lo através da construção de um plano estratégico que alavanque seus pontos fortes, se adapte à sua personalidade e maximize seus esforços de prospecção para resultados excepcionais.

DEFININDO SEUS OBJETIVOS DE PROSPECÇÃO

Comece com o fim em mente. Defina objetivos claros e mensuráveis para sua prospecção. Isso pode incluir metas relacionadas ao número de novos leads gerados, taxas de conversão de leads para clientes, ou aumento na receita. Ter objetivos específicos permite que você crie um plano direcionado e mensure seu sucesso de forma eficaz.

CONHECENDO SEUS PONTOS FORTES

Cada pessoa tem um conjunto único de habilidades e preferências. Alguns podem ser excelentes em comunicação face a face, enquanto outros podem ser mestres na escrita persuasiva. Avalie seus pontos fortes e considere como você pode utilizá-los de maneira mais eficaz em seu plano de prospecção. Por exemplo, se você é excepcional em comunicação escrita, técnicas como envio de e-mails frios podem ser mais adequadas para você.

ESCOLHENDO SUAS TÁTICAS DE PROSPECÇÃO

Com base nos seus pontos fortes e objetivos, selecione as táticas de prospecção que melhor se alinham ao seu perfil e ao seu mercado-alvo. Isso pode variar desde networking e participação em eventos até prospecção digital, como SEO ou marketing de conteúdo. Lembre-se, a qualidade é mais importante que a quantidade; é melhor escolher algumas táticas que você pode executar bem do que tentar fazer tudo de forma mediana.

CRIANDO UM CRONOGRAMA DE PROSPECÇÃO

A consistência é chave para a prospecção bem-sucedida. Crie um cronograma detalhado, incluindo quando e com que frequência você irá realizar suas atividades de prospecção. Isso pode ajudar a transformar a prospecção de uma tarefa esporádica em uma parte integrada da sua rotina diária ou semanal. Certifique-se de também alocar tempo para análise e ajustes regulares do plano.

AUTOMATIZANDO E DELEGANDO QUANDO POSSÍVEL

Procure maneiras de tornar seu processo de prospecção mais eficiente. Ferramentas de automação podem ajudar com tarefas como agendamento de e-mails, postagens em mídias sociais e rastreamento de interações com clientes. Delegar tarefas específicas a membros da equipe ou freelancers também pode liberar seu tempo para se concentrar nas atividades de prospecção que exigem seu toque pessoal.

MONITORANDO E AJUSTANDO SEU PLANO

Um plano de prospecção é um documento vivo; ele deve ser revisado e ajustado regularmente com base no desempenho e nos feedbacks recebidos. Defina intervalos regulares para avaliar o sucesso de suas táticas de prospecção e fazer as mudanças necessárias. Lembre-se de que a flexibilidade para se adaptar é uma vantagem competitiva.

Criar um plano de prospecção personalizado é um passo fundamental para transformar a prospecção ativa de uma fonte de estresse em uma estratégia de crescimento empolgante. Ao alinhar esse plano com seus objetivos, pontos fortes e preferências, você estabelece uma fundação sólida para o sucesso sustentável em vendas.

Pronto para colocar seu plano em ação? No próximo capítulo, **CHAMADA FRIA COM CONFIANÇA**, exploraremos como abordar uma das técnicas de prospecção mais tradicionais e desafiadoras com uma nova perspectiva e confiança renovada. Esteja preparado para transformar a temido chamada fria em uma ferramenta poderosa no seu arsenal de prospecção.

CHAMADA FRIA COM CONFIANÇA

Chamada fria, a prática de ligar para potenciais clientes sem um contato prévio, é frequentemente vista como uma das tarefas mais desafiadoras nas vendas. No entanto, com a abordagem certa e uma dose saudável de confiança, a chamada fria pode se transformar em uma estratégia eficaz e até gratificante. Este capítulo se destina a equipá-lo com técnicas e mentalidades que transformarão suas ligações frias de fontes de ansiedade para oportunidades de crescimento.

DESMISTIFICANDO A CHAMADA FRIA

O primeiro passo para abordar a chamada fria com confiança é mudar sua percepção sobre ele. Chamada fria não é sobre interrupção ou inconveniência; é uma oportunidade para você apresentar uma solução que pode beneficiar genuinamente seu potencial cliente. Encare cada chamada como um serviço, não como uma venda forçada.

PREPARAÇÃO É A CHAVE

Uma preparação sólida é essencial para o sucesso da chamada fria. Isso significa pesquisar sobre a empresa e a pessoa que você está ligando, entendendo seus desafios e necessidades. Crie um roteiro básico para sua chamada, mas esteja preparado para desviar dele; o roteiro deve servir como um guia, não como um script rígido.

CONSTRUINDO RAPPORT RAPIDAMENTE

Nos primeiros momentos de uma chamada fria, é crucial estabelecer uma conexão. Isso pode ser feito mencionando algo que você tenha em comum, fazendo uma observação sobre algo recente na indústria do potencial cliente ou simplesmente sendo amigável e acessível. Rapport é a fundação para a confiança e abertura durante a conversa.

FOCANDO NOS BENEFÍCIOS, NÃO NAS CARACTERÍSTICAS

Durante sua chamada, concentre-se em como seu produto ou serviço pode beneficiar o cliente. Evite a tentação de listar todas as características; em vez disso, destaque como essas características resolvem problemas específicos ou melhoram situações para o seu potencial cliente. Isso torna a conversa mais relevante e envolvente para eles.

LIDANDO COM OBJEÇÕES

Objeções são uma parte natural do processo de chamada fria. Em vez de temê-las, veja-as como oportunidades para entender melhor as preocupações do seu potencial cliente e responder de forma educada e informativa. A chave aqui é escutar ativamente, validar a preocupação do cliente e então apresentar informações que possam ajudar a superar a objeção.

MANTENDO UMA ATITUDE POSITIVA

Uma atitude positiva é contagiosa e pode fazer uma grande diferença na receptividade de sua chamada. Mesmo diante de rejeições, mantenha um tom amigável e profissional. Cada chamada é uma oportunidade de aprimorar suas habilidades, então procure aprender com a experiência, independentemente do resultado.

PRATICANDO E APERFEIÇOANDO

Como muitas habilidades, a chamada fria melhora com a prática. Não se desencoraje por rejeições ou chamadas difíceis; em vez disso, use-as como feedback para refinar sua abordagem. Considere também buscar feedback de colegas ou mentores que possam oferecer perspectivas e dicas valiosas.

A chamada fria não precisa ser uma tarefa temida. Com a preparação correta, uma mentalidade positiva e um foco genuíno em como você pode ajudar seus potenciais clientes, você pode transformar ligações frias em conversas produtivas e, eventualmente, em relações comerciais valiosas.

À medida que avançamos, o próximo capítulo, **ESTRATÉGIAS DE ENVIOS DE E-MAILS FRIOS QUE FUNCIONAM**, irá explorar como complementar suas técnicas de chamadas frias com estratégias eficazes de envios de e-mails frios, garantindo uma abordagem de prospecção abrangente e multifacetada. Prepare-se para dominar outra ferramenta vital em seu arsenal de prospecção.

ESTRATÉGIAS DE ENVIOS DE E-MAILS FRIOS QUE FUNCIONAM

O envios de e-mails frios, assim como a chamada fria, é uma ferramenta de prospecção poderosa quando utilizada corretamente. No entanto, com as caixas de entrada dos potenciais clientes frequentemente saturadas, fazer com que seu e-mail não apenas seja aberto, mas também lido e respondido, requer uma abordagem estratégica e personalizada. Este capítulo irá guiá-lo através de estratégias eficazes de envios de e-mails frios, permitindo que você crie e-mails que se destacam e geram resultados.

A IMPORTÂNCIA DA LINHA DE ASSUNTO

A linha de assunto é, sem dúvida, o elemento mais crítico do seu e-mail frio. É o primeiro ponto de contato e o principal fator que determina se o seu e-mail será aberto. As linhas de assunto devem ser claras, intrigantes e personalizadas, dando ao destinatário uma razão para clicar. Evite palavras que soem como spam e opte por frases que despertam curiosidade ou destaquem um benefício claro.

PERSONALIZAÇÃO É A CHAVE

Enviar o mesmo e-mail genérico para todos os seus contatos é uma receita para o fracasso. A personalização mostra que você dedicou tempo para conhecer o destinatário e sua empresa, aumentando as chances de engajamento. Use o nome do destinatário, referencie projetos recentes da empresa ou mencione desafios específicos do setor para criar uma conexão imediata.

FOCO NO VALOR, NÃO NA VENDA

O objetivo do seu e-mail frio não deve ser vender desde a primeira linha, mas sim iniciar uma conversa. Concentre-se em como você pode agregar valor ao destinatário ou ajudar a resolver um problema específico que eles possam estar enfrentando. Ao posicionar-se como um recurso valioso, em vez de apenas outro vendedor, você aumenta as chances de uma resposta positiva.

CLAREZA E CONCISÃO

Um e-mail frio eficaz vai direto ao ponto. Mantenha sua mensagem curta, clara e focada no valor que você está oferecendo. Cada frase deve ter um propósito, seja ele capturar a atenção, destacar um benefício ou chamar à ação. Lembre-se de que o tempo do seu destinatário é precioso, portanto, faça valer a pena.

CHAMADA À AÇÃO CLARA

Seu e-mail deve terminar com uma chamada à ação (CTA) clara e específica. Isso pode ser uma solicitação para uma reunião, uma resposta a uma pergunta específica ou uma oferta para enviar mais informações. Seja qual for a CTA, ela deve ser simples e requerer um esforço mínimo por parte do destinatário para aumentar suas chances de engajamento.

ACOMPANHAMENTO ESTRATÉGICO

O acompanhamento é uma parte crucial do processo de envios de e-mails frios. Se você não receber resposta, envie um e-mail de follow-up após alguns dias, lembrando gentilmente ao destinatário sobre sua mensagem anterior e reforçando o valor que você pode oferecer. Limitar-se a um ou dois e-mails de acompanhamento é geralmente considerado uma boa prática para evitar ser intrusivo.

TESTE E OTIMIZAÇÃO

Assim como outras formas de marketing, o envio de e-mail frio é um processo iterativo. Teste diferentes linhas de assunto, estilos de mensagem e chamadas à ação para ver o que gera a melhor resposta. Use as taxas de abertura, cliques e respostas para refinar sua abordagem ao longo do tempo.

O envio de e-mail frio, quando feito corretamente, pode ser uma estratégia de prospecção excepcionalmente eficaz. Com uma abordagem personalizada, focada no valor e clara, seus e-mails não apenas serão lidos, mas também agirão como um ponto de partida para relações comerciais valiosas.

Prosseguindo, o próximo capítulo, **UTILIZANDO AS REDES SOCIAIS PARA PROSPECÇÃO**, explorará como você pode alavancar as plataformas de mídia social para identificar e engajar potenciais clientes, complementando suas estratégias de chamadas frias e envios de e-mails com sucesso nas redes sociais. Prepare-se para expandir seu alcance e fortalecer suas estratégias de prospecção com o poder das mídias sociais.

UTILIZANDO AS REDES SOCIAIS PARA PROSPECÇÃO

As redes sociais transformaram o modo como nos conectamos, comunicamos e até como fazemos negócios. Para profissionais de vendas e pequenos empresários, elas oferecem uma plataforma dinâmica para prospecção, permitindo que você alcance potenciais clientes onde eles já estão ativos. Este capítulo foca em estratégias eficazes para utilizar as redes sociais na prospecção, ajudando você a identificar, engajar e converter potenciais clientes em um ambiente digital.

ESCOLHENDO AS PLATAFORMAS CERTAS

A primeira etapa é identificar em quais plataformas de mídia social seus potenciais clientes são mais ativos. Enquanto o LinkedIn é frequentemente a escolha padrão para prospecção B2B, plataformas como Twitter, Facebook e Instagram podem ser igualmente valiosas, dependendo do seu mercado-alvo. A chave é focar seus esforços nas plataformas que oferecem o maior retorno sobre o investimento de tempo e recursos.

CONSTRUINDO UM PERFIL ATRAENTE

Antes de começar a prospectar, é crucial que seu próprio perfil nas redes sociais esteja otimizado e profissional. Isso significa ter uma foto de perfil clara, uma bio bem escrita que destaca seu valor e experiência, e, se aplicável, um portfólio de trabalhos anteriores ou depoimentos. Seu perfil deve comunicar não apenas quem você é, mas como você pode ajudar seus potenciais clientes.

ENGAJAMENTO AUTÊNTICO

O segredo para a prospecção eficaz nas redes sociais é o engajamento autêntico. Isso pode incluir compartilhar conteúdo relevante, comentar em postagens de potenciais clientes ou participar de discussões em grupos do setor. O objetivo é construir relacionamentos genuínos, fornecendo valor e estabelecendo-se como uma autoridade no seu campo, não apenas vender seu produto ou serviço.

ESTRATÉGIAS DE CONTEÚDO

Criar e compartilhar conteúdo que seja tanto informativo quanto atraente é uma maneira poderosa de atrair potenciais clientes. Isso pode variar desde artigos de blog e estudos de caso até vídeos e infográficos. O conteúdo não só ajuda a estabelecer sua expertise, mas também oferece uma razão para os potenciais clientes se conectarem e interagirem com você.

MONITORANDO E INTERAGINDO

Use ferramentas de monitoramento de mídia social para rastrear menções da sua marca, produtos, serviços ou palavras-chave relevantes do setor. Isso não só ajuda a identificar oportunidades de prospecção, mas também permite que você interaja proativamente com potenciais clientes, respondendo a perguntas, oferecendo soluções ou simplesmente agradecendo por menções ou compartilhamentos.

APROVEITANDO ANÚNCIOS PAGOS

As plataformas de mídia social oferecem opções robustas de publicidade paga que podem ser usadas para segmentar especificamente seu público-alvo com mensagens personalizadas. Seja através de anúncios no LinkedIn para alcançar profissionais de um determinado setor ou campanhas no Facebook para atingir um público com interesses específicos, os anúncios pagos podem ser uma forma eficiente de aumentar seu alcance e gerar leads qualificados.

MENSURANDO SEU SUCESSO

Como em todas as estratégias de vendas e marketing, a mensuração é fundamental para entender o que está funcionando e o que precisa ser ajustado. Use as ferramentas de análise fornecidas pelas plataformas de mídia social para rastrear o engajamento, o crescimento do público e a conversão de leads. Esses dados fornecerão insights valiosos para otimizar sua abordagem de prospecção.

A prospecção nas redes sociais, quando feita corretamente, pode ser uma forma eficaz de construir relacionamentos e gerar leads. Ao combinar um perfil otimizado, engajamento autêntico, conteúdo de valor e monitoramento proativo, você pode transformar as redes sociais em um canal poderoso para o crescimento do seu negócio.

Avançando, o próximo capítulo, **GESTÃO DO TEMPO PARA PROSPECÇÃO**, abordará como organizar sua agenda para maximizar o tempo dedicado à prospecção, garantindo que você possa efetivamente balancear essa atividade essencial com outras responsabilidades do seu negócio. Prepare-se para aprender a gerir seu tempo de forma que potencialize suas estratégias de prospecção.

GESTÃO DO TEMPO PARA PROSPECÇÃO

A prospecção é uma atividade crucial que alimenta o funil de vendas e sustenta o crescimento do negócio. No entanto, sem uma gestão de tempo eficaz, pode-se facilmente cair na armadilha de deixar a prospecção de lado em favor de tarefas mais imediatas ou confortáveis. Este capítulo se dedica a estratégias de gestão do tempo que garantem a alocação adequada de recursos para a prospecção, equilibrando-a com outras importantes responsabilidades diárias.

ESTABELECENDO PRIORIDADES

Comece identificando a prospecção como uma de suas principais prioridades. Isso significa reconhecer conscientemente o valor da prospecção para o sucesso a longo prazo do seu negócio e comprometer-se a dedicar um tempo regular a essa atividade. Lembre-se, a prospecção não é apenas uma tarefa adicional; é o motor que impulsiona o crescimento.

BLOCOS DE TEMPO DEDICADOS

Uma técnica eficaz de gestão do tempo é o uso de blocos de tempo dedicados exclusivamente à prospecção. Isso pode ser algumas horas diárias ou blocos de tempo específicos ao longo da semana. Durante esses períodos, minimize as distrações e foque totalmente nas atividades de prospecção. A regularidade e a consistência são chaves para transformar a prospecção em um hábito produtivo.

AUTOMATIZAÇÃO E FERRAMENTAS

A tecnologia pode ser uma grande aliada na economia de tempo durante o processo de prospecção. Use ferramentas de automação para tarefas repetitivas, como o envio de e-mails de acompanhamento ou a publicação em mídias sociais. Além disso, utilize CRMs (Customer Relationship Management) para organizar leads, monitorar interações e programar lembretes para follow-ups.

TAREFAS AGRUPADAS

Agrupar tarefas semelhantes pode aumentar significativamente a eficiência. Dedique blocos de tempo para atividades específicas, como pesquisa de potenciais clientes, envio de e-mails, realização de chamadas telefônicas ou atualização do seu CRM. Isso ajuda a manter o foco e reduzir o tempo perdido na transição entre diferentes tipos de tarefas.

DELEGAÇÃO

Considere delegar atividades que não exigem sua atenção direta. Isso pode incluir a qualificação inicial de leads, a gestão de perfis de mídia social ou até mesmo a pesquisa de mercado. Delegar tarefas a membros da equipe ou assistentes virtuais pode liberar seu tempo para se concentrar em atividades de prospecção de alto valor.

ESTABELECENDO METAS CLARAS

Defina metas claras e mensuráveis para suas atividades de prospecção. Isso pode incluir um número específico de novos contatos por semana, uma quantidade de e-mails de prospecção enviados ou um número de chamadas frias realizadas. As metas ajudam a manter o foco e oferecem um critério claro para avaliar seu progresso.

REVISÃO E AJUSTE

Faça revisões regulares de sua gestão do tempo e das atividades de prospecção. Isso envolve analisar o que está funcionando, o que não está e ajustar sua abordagem conforme necessário. A adaptabilidade é crucial, pois permite otimizar sua eficácia e garantir que seu tempo seja sempre bem investido.

A gestão eficaz do tempo na prospecção não apenas assegura que essa atividade crucial receba a atenção devida, mas também maximiza a eficácia de seus esforços. Implementando estratégias sólidas de gestão do tempo, você pode garantir que a prospecção ocupe seu merecido lugar como uma prioridade inabalável no seu dia a dia de negócios.

Prosseguindo, o próximo capítulo, **RESPONDENDO A OBJEÇÕES**, mergulhará nas estratégias para transformar objeções em oportunidades, ajudando você a superar barreiras e avançar nas conversas de vendas. Esteja preparado para abordar as objeções não como obstáculos, mas como degraus para o sucesso nas vendas.

RESPONDENDO A OBJEÇÕES

Enfrentar objeções é uma parte natural do processo de vendas. Ao invés de vê-las como barreiras ao sucesso, é possível transformá-las em oportunidades para aprofundar o entendimento das necessidades do cliente e reforçar o valor da sua oferta. Este capítulo explora estratégias para responder a objeções de maneira eficaz, ajudando você a navegar por esses momentos críticos e avançar na conversa de vendas com confiança.

ENTENDENDO AS OBJEÇÕES

O primeiro passo para responder eficazmente a uma objeção é entender sua origem. Muitas vezes, objeções surgem de uma falta de informação ou compreensão, preocupações com o custo ou valor, ou simplesmente resistência à mudança. Ouvir atentamente e fazer perguntas esclarecedoras pode ajudá-lo a identificar a raiz da objeção e abordá-la de maneira direcionada.

ENCARANDO OBJEÇÕES COMO OPORTUNIDADES

Cada objeção oferece uma oportunidade para aprender mais sobre o que seu potencial cliente valoriza ou preocupa. Além disso, abordar objeções de maneira positiva e construtiva pode fortalecer a relação de confiança, demonstrando que você está genuinamente interessado em encontrar a melhor solução para as necessidades dele.

ESTRUTURA PARA RESPONDER OBJEÇÕES

Uma estrutura eficaz para responder a objeções segue quatro etapas principais:

- **Ouvir:** Dê ao cliente a oportunidade de expressar completamente sua objeção sem interrupções.

- **Clarificar:** Faça perguntas para entender completamente a objeção. Isso também mostra que você está ouvindo e se importa com suas preocupações.

- **Responder:** Aborde a objeção diretamente, fornecendo informações, exemplos e testemunhos que possam ajudar a mitigar a preocupação.

- **Confirmar:** Verifique se a sua resposta satisfaz a objeção do cliente e se há mais alguma dúvida.

PERSONALIZE SUA RESPOSTA

Embora seja útil ter respostas preparadas para objeções comuns, a personalização é crucial. Use o que você sabe sobre as necessidades e desejos específicos do cliente para moldar sua resposta. Isso não só torna sua resposta mais relevante, mas também demonstra um compromisso em fornecer uma solução verdadeiramente personalizada.

RESPOSTAS BASEADAS EM VALOR

Quando os clientes expressam preocupações sobre o preço, é uma oportunidade para reforçar o valor do seu produto ou serviço. Explique como os benefícios superam o custo e como a oferta pode economizar tempo, dinheiro ou outros recursos no longo prazo. Histórias de sucesso de clientes similares podem ser particularmente persuasivas neste contexto.

PRATIQUE E PREPARE-SE

A prática leva à perfeição. Reúna objeções comuns no seu setor e pratique suas respostas. Isso não apenas o ajudará a se sentir mais confiante durante as conversas de vendas, mas também garantirá que suas respostas sejam coerentes, informativas e convincentes.

MANTENHA A CONVERSA AVANÇANDO

Finalmente, após abordar uma objeção, é importante redirecionar a conversa de volta para o caminho da venda. Faça uma pergunta aberta que permita ao cliente expressar quaisquer outras preocupações ou retorne ao diálogo sobre os benefícios e vantagens da sua oferta.

Responder a objeções não é um obstáculo, mas uma parte integrante do processo de vendas que, quando manejada corretamente, pode aproximar você do fechamento da venda. Encare cada objeção como uma chance de aprofundar o relacionamento com o cliente e solidificar a confiança na sua oferta.

À medida que avançamos, o próximo capítulo, **SEGUINDO SEM SER INVASIVO**, focará em como equilibrar a persistência e a cortesia no acompanhamento com potenciais clientes, garantindo que você mantenha a conexão sem ultrapassar limites. Prepare-se para aprender a arte de seguir em frente de maneira respeitosa e eficaz.

SEGUINDO SEM SER INVASIVO

O acompanhamento é uma etapa crucial no processo de vendas, mas encontrar o equilíbrio certo para não se tornar invasivo pode ser desafiador. Este capítulo aborda estratégias eficazes para manter o interesse e avançar a conversa com potenciais clientes, respeitando seus limites e tempos.

A IMPORTÂNCIA DO TIMING

O timing é tudo quando se trata de seguir em frente. Demorar muito para entrar em contato pode fazer com que o lead esfrie, mas ser rápido demais pode parecer pressão de venda. A chave está em estabelecer um cronograma razoável baseado em pistas do cliente e normas do setor. Após o primeiro contato ou apresentação, dar espaço de alguns dias antes do primeiro follow-up pode ser um bom ponto de partida.

PERSONALIZE SEUS FOLLOW-UPS

Cada interação com um potencial cliente deve ser personalizada para refletir conversas anteriores, seus interesses específicos e qualquer objeção que tenha sido levantada. Isso demonstra que você está atento às suas necessidades e preocupações, e não apenas enviando mensagens genéricas. A personalização aumenta a relevância do seu follow-up e a probabilidade de uma resposta positiva.

FORNECER VALOR EM CADA INTERAÇÃO

Cada follow-up deve oferecer valor adicional ao potencial cliente. Isso pode ser na forma de insights do setor, artigos relevantes, estudos de caso ou demonstrações de como seu produto ou serviço pode resolver um problema específico que eles enfrentam. Fornecer valor continuamente reforça a percepção de que você está interessado em ajudar, não apenas em vender.

UTILIZE MÚLTIPLOS CANAIS DE COMUNICAÇÃO

Diversificar os canais de comunicação pode ajudar a manter o acompanhamento fresco e menos intrusivo. Além do e-mail, considere usar chamadas telefônicas, mensagens no LinkedIn, ou até notas manuscritas, dependendo do relacionamento e preferências do cliente. O importante é respeitar as preferências do cliente sobre como eles gostariam de ser contatados.

A ARTE DE PERGUNTAR

Encoraje o diálogo fazendo perguntas abertas em seus follow-ups. Isso não apenas fornece ao cliente uma oportunidade fácil de responder, mas também pode revelar informações valiosas sobre suas hesitações ou necessidades. Perguntas como "Há alguma informação adicional que posso fornecer para ajudar na sua decisão?" convidam à interação sem pressão.

SAIBA QUANDO RECUAR

Reconhecer quando parar de insistir é tão importante quanto saber quando seguir em frente. Se um potencial cliente expressa claramente que não está interessado ou pede para não ser contatado novamente, respeite seu pedido. Manter uma atitude profissional e cortês deixa a porta aberta para futuras interações, caso as circunstâncias mudem.

MONITORANDO E AJUSTANDO SEU APROXIMAÇÃO

Acompanhar suas taxas de resposta e ajustar suas estratégias de follow-up com base no que funciona é fundamental. Anote quais abordagens geram mais engajamento e esteja disposto a experimentar novas técnicas para melhorar sua eficácia.

Seguir em frente sem ser invasivo é um equilíbrio delicado que requer atenção aos detalhes, personalização e respeito pelas preferências e limites do cliente. Implementando as estratégias acima, você pode manter uma comunicação eficaz que avança a venda sem comprometer a relação com o cliente.

Prosseguindo, o próximo capítulo, **USANDO CONTEÚDO PARA ATRAIR CLIENTES**, mergulhará na criação e uso estratégico de conteúdo para apoiar seus esforços de prospecção, atraindo clientes potenciais através da demonstração de valor e conhecimento. Prepare-se para explorar como o marketing de conteúdo pode ser uma ferramenta poderosa em seu arsenal de vendas.

USANDO CONTEÚDO PARA ATRAIR CLIENTES

No cenário atual de vendas e marketing, o conteúdo desempenha um papel fundamental na atração e engajamento de clientes potenciais. Ao oferecer informações valiosas e relevantes, você não só estabelece sua marca como uma autoridade no setor, mas também cria um caminho para que clientes potenciais venham até você. Este capítulo explora como utilizar estrategicamente o conteúdo para apoiar seus esforços de prospecção e atrair clientes.

DEFININDO SUA ESTRATÉGIA DE CONTEÚDO

Antes de começar a criar conteúdo, é importante definir uma estratégia clara. Isso inclui entender seu público-alvo, identificar os tópicos que são mais relevantes para eles e determinar os melhores canais para distribuir seu conteúdo. Sua estratégia de conteúdo deve alinhar-se com seus objetivos de prospecção e vendas, visando resolver problemas ou responder perguntas que seus clientes potenciais possam ter.

TIPOS DE CONTEÚDO PARA ATRAIR CLIENTES

- **Blog posts:** Artigos informativos que abordam tópicos relevantes para seu público podem ajudar a melhorar sua visibilidade nos motores de busca e estabelecer sua marca como um recurso valioso.

- **E-books e whitepapers:** Conteúdo mais longo e detalhado pode ser usado para gerar leads, pedindo aos visitantes que forneçam suas informações de contato em troca do download.

- **Vídeos:** Vídeos explicativos, depoimentos de clientes e visões gerais de produtos são altamente engajadores e podem ser compartilhados facilmente nas mídias sociais.

- **Infográficos:** Informações complexas apresentadas de maneira visual e acessível podem ajudar a captar a atenção e facilitar o compartilhamento online.

- **Webinars:** Sessões educativas online podem ser uma

excelente maneira de demonstrar sua expertise e interagir diretamente com clientes potenciais.

PROMOVENDO SEU CONTEÚDO

Criar conteúdo valioso é apenas metade da batalha; promovê-lo eficazmente é igualmente importante. Utilize as mídias sociais, e-mails, SEO e até parcerias com influenciadores ou outras marcas para ampliar o alcance do seu conteúdo. A promoção cruzada entre diferentes canais pode aumentar significativamente a visibilidade e o engajamento.

MENSURANDO O SUCESSO DO CONTEÚDO

Para entender o impacto do seu conteúdo, é crucial acompanhar métricas como tráfego no site, engajamento nas mídias sociais, downloads de recursos e, mais importante, conversões em leads. Essas informações ajudarão a refinar sua estratégia de conteúdo e focar nos tipos de conteúdo que geram os melhores resultados.

CONTEÚDO COMO FERRAMENTA DE PROSPECÇÃO

Além de atrair clientes potenciais, o conteúdo pode ser usado ativamente na prospecção. Incluir links para conteúdo relevante em e-mails frios ou mensagens de mídia social pode agregar valor à sua comunicação e aumentar as taxas de resposta. O conteúdo também pode ser um excelente ponto de partida para discussões durante chamadas de vendas ou reuniões.

CONSTRUINDO RELACIONAMENTOS ATRAVÉS DO CONTEÚDO

Finalmente, o conteúdo não é apenas uma ferramenta para atrair clientes, mas também para construir e nutrir relacionamentos com eles. Ao fornecer conteúdo consistente e valioso, você mantém sua marca na mente dos clientes e estabelece uma base de confiança que pode levar a relacionamentos comerciais duradouros.

O uso estratégico de conteúdo para atrair clientes é uma abordagem poderosa na era digital. Ao criar e promover conteúdo que ressoa com seu público-alvo, você pode não apenas aumentar sua visibilidade e autoridade, mas também gerar leads qualificados e estabelecer relacionamentos significativos com clientes potenciais.

Avançando, o próximo capítulo, **ESTRATÉGIAS DE SEO PARA GERAÇÃO DE LEADS**, irá mergulhar em como otimizar sua presença online para ser encontrado por clientes em potencial, garantindo que seu conteúdo e sua marca alcancem o público certo no momento certo. Prepare-se para explorar o poder do SEO na sua estratégia de prospecção.

ESTRATÉGIAS DE SEO PARA GERAÇÃO DE LEADS

A otimização para motores de busca (SEO) é uma ferramenta poderosa para melhorar a visibilidade online da sua marca e atrair clientes potenciais de maneira orgânica. A chave para uma estratégia de SEO eficaz é garantir que seu conteúdo e site sejam encontrados por clientes em potencial no momento em que estão buscando soluções que você oferece. Este capítulo explora estratégias de SEO fundamentais para melhorar sua geração de leads.

COMPREENDENDO O SEO

SEO envolve uma série de práticas destinadas a melhorar a posição do seu site nos resultados de pesquisa para termos e frases relevantes. Isso é conseguido através da otimização de diversos elementos do seu site, incluindo conteúdo, estrutura, meta tags, links internos e externos, entre outros. O objetivo é tornar o seu site mais atraente para os motores de busca e para os usuários.

PESQUISA DE PALAVRAS-CHAVE

O primeiro passo em qualquer estratégia de SEO é a pesquisa de palavras-chave. Isso envolve identificar os termos que seu público-alvo utiliza quando busca por informações, produtos ou serviços relacionados ao seu negócio. Ferramentas como Google Keyword Planner e SEMrush podem ajudar a identificar essas palavras-chave, bem como o volume de pesquisa e a concorrência por elas.

OTIMIZAÇÃO ON-PAGE

Uma vez que você tenha identificado suas palavras-chave alvo, o próximo passo é integrá-las ao seu site. Isso inclui a otimização de títulos, meta descrições, cabeçalhos, e o próprio conteúdo das páginas para incluir suas palavras-chave de forma natural e relevante. Além disso, assegure que seu site tenha uma estrutura lógica e fácil de navegar, tanto para usuários quanto para motores de busca.

CONTEÚDO DE QUALIDADE

O conteúdo é o coração do SEO. Produzir conteúdo original, valioso e relevante não só atrai visitantes ao seu site, mas também encoraja outros sites a linkarem para o seu, o que pode melhorar significativamente seu ranking nos motores de busca. Blogs, estudos de caso, e-books, infográficos e vídeos são todos formatos de conteúdo que podem ser otimizados para SEO.

SEO TÉCNICO

SEO técnico refere-se à otimização da infraestrutura do seu site para garantir que ele seja indexado e ranqueado efetivamente pelos motores de busca. Isso inclui melhorar a velocidade do site, garantir que o site seja mobile-friendly, utilizar SSL, otimizar URLs, e criar um arquivo sitemap.xml para ajudar os motores de busca a rastrearem seu site mais facilmente.

LINK BUILDING

Construir um perfil de backlink forte é outro componente crucial do SEO. Isso envolve obter links de outros sites de autoridade para o seu. Estratégias para conseguir isso incluem a criação de conteúdo compartilhável, guest blogging, e a participação em diretórios de negócios relevantes. Links de qualidade indicam aos motores de busca que seu site é uma fonte confiável de informação.

MENSURAÇÃO E AJUSTE

Por fim, é crucial monitorar o desempenho do seu site nos motores de busca e ajustar sua estratégia conforme necessário. Ferramentas como Google Analytics e Google Search Console podem fornecer insights valiosos sobre o tráfego do site, conversões, e o desempenho de suas palavras-chave, permitindo que você refine continuamente sua abordagem de SEO para melhorar a geração de leads.

Uma estratégia de SEO bem executada pode significativamente aumentar a visibilidade do seu site, atrair tráfego qualificado e gerar leads de maneira orgânica. Ao focar na pesquisa de palavras-chave, otimização on-page, conteúdo de qualidade, SEO técnico, e link building, você pode melhorar seu ranking nos motores de busca e capturar a atenção de clientes potenciais no momento certo.

Avançando, o próximo capítulo, **FERRAMENTAS DIGITAIS E AUTOMAÇÃO EM PROSPECÇÃO**, explorará como a tecnologia pode simplificar e tornar mais eficientes suas estratégias de prospecção, permitindo que você se concentre em construir relações e fechar vendas. Prepare-se para descobrir ferramentas que podem transformar sua abordagem de prospecção.

FERRAMENTAS DIGITAIS E AUTOMAÇÃO EM PROSPECÇÃO

No mundo digital de hoje, a tecnologia oferece uma infinidade de ferramentas que podem otimizar e automatizar muitos aspectos da prospecção, tornando o processo mais eficiente e permitindo que você dedique mais tempo à interação humana significativa. Este capítulo explora as ferramentas digitais e a automação em prospecção, destacando como elas podem transformar suas estratégias de prospecção.

CRM (CUSTOMER RELATIONSHIP MANAGEMENT)

Sistemas de CRM são o coração da prospecção digital, permitindo que você organize, acompanhe e gerencie leads e clientes em todo o ciclo de vendas. Eles fornecem uma visão 360 graus de suas interações com clientes, histórico de compras, preferências e muito mais, facilitando a personalização da abordagem de vendas e a identificação de oportunidades de upsell e cross-sell.

AUTOMAÇÃO DE E-MAIL

A automação de e-mail permite que você envie e-mails personalizados para listas segmentadas de contatos com base em ações específicas, como visitar uma página do seu site, baixar um recurso ou abandonar um carrinho de compras. Campanhas de nutrição de leads podem ser automatizadas para entregar conteúdo relevante em intervalos programados, movendo leads pelo funil de vendas de forma eficiente.

FERRAMENTAS DE PROSPECÇÃO E PESQUISA

Existem várias ferramentas disponíveis projetadas especificamente para ajudar na identificação e pesquisa de potenciais clientes. Essas ferramentas podem fornecer informações valiosas como detalhes de contato, tamanho da empresa, setor de atuação e até sinais de compra, permitindo que você personalize sua abordagem de prospecção e direcione esforços para os leads mais promissores.

AUTOMAÇÃO DE AGENDAMENTO

Ferramentas de agendamento automatizado, como Calendly ou HubSpot Meetings, permitem que potenciais clientes agendem reuniões ou chamadas com você sem a necessidade de trocas intermináveis de e-mails. Essas ferramentas podem ser integradas ao seu calendário, mostrando sua disponibilidade em tempo real e automatizando lembretes de reuniões, melhorando a experiência do cliente e economizando tempo.

SOCIAL SELLING E FERRAMENTAS DE MONITORAMENTO

O social selling é uma estratégia importante na prospecção moderna. Ferramentas de monitoramento de mídia social permitem que você acompanhe menções da sua marca, palavras-chave relevantes e atividades dos concorrentes. Além disso, plataformas como LinkedIn Sales Navigator são projetadas para ajudar na prospecção B2B, oferecendo recursos avançados de pesquisa e recomendações personalizadas de leads.

ANÁLISE E RELATÓRIOS

Ferramentas de análise e relatórios fornecem insights valiosos sobre o desempenho das suas estratégias de prospecção, desde a eficácia de campanhas de e-mail até o engajamento nas redes sociais e conversões no site. Esses dados permitem que você ajuste suas táticas em tempo real, concentrando esforços nas atividades que geram os melhores resultados.

CONSIDERAÇÕES DE PRIVACIDADE E CONFORMIDADE

Ao implementar ferramentas digitais e automação, é vital considerar questões de privacidade e conformidade, especialmente em relação a regulamentos como o GDPR. Garanta que suas práticas estejam em conformidade e que a privacidade dos dados do cliente seja sempre priorizada.

As ferramentas digitais e a automação em prospecção não são apenas sobre eficiência; elas são sobre melhorar a qualidade das interações com clientes potenciais e personalizar a jornada de vendas para suas necessidades específicas. Ao adotar essas tecnologias, você pode transformar sua abordagem de prospecção, criando mais oportunidades de vendas e construindo relações mais fortes com clientes.

O próximo capítulo, **CRIANDO E MANTENDO RELACIONAMENTOS DURADOUROS COM CLIENTES**, se aprofundará em como nutrir esses contatos iniciais em relacionamentos duradouros e lucrativos, utilizando as ferramentas e estratégias discutidas para maximizar o valor do cliente a longo prazo. Prepare-se para descobrir o segredo para transformar leads em clientes fiéis.

CRIANDO E MANTENDO RELACIONAMENTOS DURADOUROS COM CLIENTES

A construção de relacionamentos duradouros com clientes vai além da conversão de vendas. É sobre cultivar confiança, oferecer valor contínuo e criar uma experiência positiva que incentive a lealdade do cliente a longo prazo. Este capítulo foca em estratégias eficazes para não apenas ganhar novos clientes, mas manter esses relacionamentos crescendo e prosperando ao longo do tempo.

CONHECENDO SEUS CLIENTES

Um relacionamento duradouro começa com um entendimento profundo de quem são seus clientes, suas necessidades, desejos, desafios e como seus produtos ou serviços se encaixam em suas vidas. Utilize dados coletados durante o processo de vendas, feedback direto e interações para criar perfis detalhados de cliente, permitindo que você personalize suas comunicações e ofertas.

COMUNICAÇÃO CONSISTENTE E PERSONALIZADA

Mantenha uma comunicação regular com seus clientes, mas assegure que cada interação traga valor. Use os dados coletados para personalizar suas mensagens, seja através de e-mails personalizados, ofertas exclusivas ou conteúdo relevante. Lembre-se, a personalização é chave para fazer o cliente se sentir valorizado e compreendido.

FORNECER SUPORTE EXCEPCIONAL

Um excelente serviço ao cliente é fundamental para manter relacionamentos duradouros. Isso significa não apenas resolver problemas rapidamente, mas também superar expectativas sempre que possível. Disponibilize múltiplos canais de suporte, treine sua equipe para ser empática e solícita, e sempre busque feedback para melhorar.

RECOMPENSAR A LEALDADE

Programas de fidelidade e recompensas podem ser uma maneira eficaz de incentivar e agradecer aos clientes pela sua contínua patronagem. Ofertas exclusivas, descontos, acesso antecipado a novos produtos ou serviços, e reconhecimento em plataformas de mídia social são todas formas de mostrar apreço e reforçar a lealdade do cliente.

ENVOLVER CLIENTES NA EVOLUÇÃO DO PRODUTO

Clientes se sentem mais engajados e valorizados quando têm voz ativa no desenvolvimento de produtos ou serviços. Considere implementar programas de feedback do cliente ou grupos focais para coletar insights que podem orientar inovações ou melhorias. Comunicar como o feedback do cliente contribuiu para mudanças também pode fortalecer o relacionamento.

ACOMPANHAMENTO PÓS-VENDA

O relacionamento com o cliente não termina na venda. Acompanhamentos pós-venda para verificar a satisfação do cliente e oferecer suporte adicional podem transformar uma venda única em um relacionamento contínuo. Isso também pode ser uma oportunidade para coletar feedback valioso e identificar oportunidades para vendas adicionais ou cross-selling.

CONSTRUIR UMA COMUNIDADE

Criar uma comunidade em torno da sua marca pode fomentar um sentido de pertencimento entre seus clientes. Isso pode ser feito através de fóruns online, grupos de mídia social ou eventos exclusivos para clientes. Uma comunidade ativa não apenas apoia os clientes existentes, mas também pode atrair novos clientes através de referências e recomendações.

ESTAR PRESENTE E DISPONÍVEL

Por fim, estar presente e acessível para seus clientes comunica que você valoriza o relacionamento. Seja responsivo nas mídias sociais, ofereça canais de comunicação direta e esteja disponível para conversar e resolver quaisquer questões que surjam.

Criar e manter relacionamentos duradouros com clientes é um investimento contínuo no sucesso a longo prazo do seu negócio.

Ao focar em conhecer seus clientes, personalizar a comunicação, fornecer suporte excepcional e envolvê-los na jornada da sua marca, você pode construir uma base de clientes leais que não apenas continuará comprando de você, mas também se tornará advogada da sua marca.

Prosseguindo, o próximo capítulo, **MEDINDO O SUCESSO DA SUA PROSPECÇÃO**, detalhará como identificar e utilizar indicadores-chave de desempenho (KPIs) para avaliar e refinar suas estratégias de prospecção e relacionamento com clientes, garantindo que seus esforços estejam alinhados com os objetivos de crescimento do seu negócio. Prepare-se para aprender a mensurar o sucesso de suas iniciativas de forma eficaz.

MEDINDO O SUCESSO DA SUA PROSPECÇÃO

Para garantir que suas estratégias de prospecção e relacionamento com clientes sejam eficazes e estejam contribuindo para o crescimento do seu negócio, é crucial medir o sucesso dessas iniciativas. Este capítulo discute como identificar, monitorar e utilizar indicadores-chave de desempenho (KPIs) para avaliar a eficácia de suas técnicas de prospecção e ajustar suas estratégias conforme necessário.

ESTABELECENDO KPIS DE PROSPECÇÃO

Os KPIs de prospecção devem estar alinhados com os objetivos gerais de vendas e marketing do seu negócio. Alguns KPIs fundamentais incluem:

- **Taxa de conversão de leads:** A porcentagem de leads que se convertem em clientes pagantes. Esse indicador pode ajudar a avaliar a qualidade dos leads gerados por suas atividades de prospecção.

- **Custo por lead (CPL):** O custo total de geração de leads dividido pelo número total de leads. Este KPI é crucial para avaliar a eficiência de seus esforços de marketing e prospecção.

- **Taxa de resposta:** A porcentagem de contatos que respondem às suas tentativas de prospecção, como e-mails ou chamadas. Uma taxa de resposta baixa pode indicar a necessidade de ajustar sua mensagem ou abordagem.

- **Tempo para o fechamento:** O tempo médio necessário para converter um lead em cliente. Este KPI pode ajudar a identificar gargalos no processo de vendas.

- **Valor do ciclo de vida do cliente (CLV):** A receita total esperada de um cliente ao longo de seu relacionamento com a empresa. Este indicador destaca a importância de manter relacionamentos duradouros com clientes.

MONITORANDO E ANALISANDO OS DADOS

Com os KPIs estabelecidos, o próximo passo é implementar sistemas para coletar e analisar esses dados. Ferramentas de CRM, automação de marketing e plataformas de análise web podem fornecer insights valiosos sobre o desempenho de suas atividades de prospecção. Monitore esses KPIs regularmente para identificar tendências, sucessos e áreas que requerem atenção.

AJUSTANDO ESTRATÉGIAS BASEADO EM DADOS

A análise dos KPIs pode revelar insights cruciais que permitem ajustar suas estratégias de prospecção para melhorar o desempenho. Por exemplo, se a taxa de conversão de leads for baixa, isso pode indicar a necessidade de revisar seu público-alvo ou sua proposta de valor. Se o CPL estiver alto, explore maneiras de otimizar suas campanhas de marketing para reduzir custos.

TESTES A/B

Implementar testes A/B em suas campanhas de prospecção pode ajudar a determinar quais estratégias, mensagens ou canais são mais eficazes. Compare diferentes abordagens para ver qual delas gera melhores resultados em termos de taxas de conversão, resposta e engajamento.

OUVINDO O FEEDBACK DOS CLIENTES

Além dos KPIs quantitativos, o feedback qualitativo dos clientes é uma fonte rica de insights. Pesquisas de satisfação do cliente, feedback pós-venda e revisões podem fornecer informações valiosas sobre como melhorar sua abordagem de prospecção e fortalecer os relacionamentos com clientes.

Medir o sucesso da sua prospecção é fundamental para entender o impacto de suas estratégias no crescimento do negócio. Ao estabelecer KPIs claros, monitorar regularmente o desempenho e ajustar suas táticas com base em dados concretos e feedback dos clientes, você pode otimizar suas atividades de prospecção para alcançar resultados melhores e mais sustentáveis.

À medida que avançamos, o próximo capítulo, **MANEIRAS CRIATIVAS PARA GERAR LEADS**, explorará estratégias inovadoras para identificar e capturar leads, encorajando você a pensar fora da caixa em suas próprias iniciativas de prospecção. Prepare-se para descobrir abordagens únicas que podem diferenciar sua empresa e atrair mais clientes potenciais.

MANEIRAS CRIATIVAS PARA GERAR LEADS

A geração de leads é o motor que impulsiona o crescimento dos negócios, mas em um mercado cada vez mais saturado, destacar-se da concorrência exige criatividade e inovação. Este capítulo apresenta estratégias não convencionais e criativas para gerar leads, incentivando você a explorar novas abordagens para atrair clientes potenciais.

GAMIFICAÇÃO PARA ENGAJAMENTO

Incorporar elementos de jogos em sua estratégia de marketing pode aumentar significativamente o engajamento e capturar informações de leads de maneira divertida. Por exemplo, criar um quiz interativo relacionado ao seu setor, onde os participantes fornecem seu e-mail para ver os resultados, pode ser uma maneira eficaz de gerar leads qualificados enquanto oferece valor.

PARCERIAS COM INFLUENCIADORES DE NICHO

Colaborar com influenciadores que tenham um público-alvo semelhante ao seu pode abrir seu negócio para uma base de clientes completamente nova. A chave é escolher influenciadores cujos valores e público se alinhem bem com sua marca, garantindo que a parceria seja autêntica e atraente para ambas as audiências.

EVENTOS VIRTUAIS TEMÁTICOS

Organizar eventos virtuais, como webinars, workshops ou até mesmo happy hours virtuais temáticos, pode ser uma maneira excelente de gerar interesse e coletar informações de leads. Esses eventos não só posicionam sua marca como um líder de pensamento em seu setor, mas também criam um ambiente propício para a interação direta com potenciais clientes.

CONCURSOS E SORTEIOS NAS REDES SOCIAIS

Concursos e sorteios são técnicas comprovadas para gerar engajamento e capturar leads. Ao solicitar que os participantes sigam suas páginas, compartilhem seu conteúdo ou marquem amigos, você não apenas expande seu alcance, mas também coleta dados valiosos de contato para futuras campanhas de marketing.

OFERTAS EXCLUSIVAS PARA SEGUIDORES

Criar ofertas exclusivas para seus seguidores nas redes sociais ou assinantes de newsletter pode motivar o compartilhamento e a inscrição, gerando novos leads. Seja um desconto especial, acesso antecipado a produtos ou conteúdo exclusivo, essas ofertas incentivam a ação e reforçam a lealdade à marca.

MARKETING DE CONTEÚDO INTERATIVO

Desenvolver conteúdo interativo, como calculadoras online, infográficos interativos ou ebooks dinâmicos, pode ser uma forma eficaz de atrair leads. Esse tipo de conteúdo não só é mais envolvente, mas também pode ser personalizado para coletar informações específicas dos usuários, auxiliando na qualificação de leads.

PARCERIAS COM OUTRAS EMPRESAS

Identifique empresas não concorrentes que ofereçam produtos ou serviços complementares ao seu e explore oportunidades de promoção cruzada. Isso pode incluir trocas de conteúdo, pacotes de produtos compartilhados ou eventos conjuntos, ampliando o alcance de ambas as empresas e acessando novos grupos de clientes potenciais.

MARKETING DE INDICAÇÃO

Encorajar seus clientes existentes a referenciarem novos clientes pode ser uma das formas mais eficazes e de baixo custo de gerar leads. Ofereça incentivos para ambos, o que indica e o indicado, para motivar a participação e garantir que ambos vejam valor na transação.

Gerar leads requer uma combinação de estratégia, criatividade e disposição para experimentar novas abordagens. Ao implementar essas ideias criativas, você pode não apenas aumentar sua base de leads, mas também fortalecer a presença da marca e construir relacionamentos mais significativos com seus clientes.

O próximo capítulo, **VENDENDO SEM VENDER**, focará em como abordar a prospecção e as vendas de uma maneira que minimize a pressão e maximize o valor para seus clientes potenciais, criando uma experiência mais autêntica e satisfatória para ambas as partes. Prepare-se para explorar técnicas que permitem vender de maneira mais eficaz, mantendo a integridade e a autenticidade em todas as interações.

VENDENDO SEM VENDER

A arte de vender sem parecer que está vendendo, também conhecida como venda consultiva ou venda baseada em valor, é uma habilidade crucial na construção de relacionamentos duradouros e na obtenção de sucesso sustentável em vendas. Este capítulo explora como você pode abordar a prospecção e as vendas de uma maneira que naturalmente conduza à conversão, sem pressionar diretamente o cliente, criando uma experiência autêntica e satisfatória para ambas as partes.

FOCANDO NA SOLUÇÃO, NÃO NO PRODUTO

Uma abordagem eficaz é concentrar-se em entender os problemas ou necessidades do cliente e, então, apresentar sua oferta como a solução. Isso significa escutar ativamente durante as conversas, fazer perguntas pertinentes para aprofundar seu entendimento e, em seguida, personalizar sua comunicação para mostrar como seu produto ou serviço pode atender às necessidades específicas do cliente.

CONSTRUINDO RELACIONAMENTOS, NÃO FAZENDO TRANSAÇÕES

Priorize o relacionamento em longo prazo em vez de focar na transação imediata. Demonstre interesse genuíno pelo sucesso do cliente e esteja disposto a oferecer ajuda ou aconselhamento, mesmo que não resulte imediatamente em uma venda. Essa abordagem constrói confiança e credibilidade, aumentando as chances de o cliente vir a você quando estiver pronto para comprar.

EDUCAÇÃO COMO FERRAMENTA DE VENDAS

Oferecer conteúdo educativo que ajude o cliente a entender melhor seu próprio problema e as possíveis soluções pode ser uma forma poderosa de vender sem vender. Webinars, e-books, estudos de caso e blogs são ferramentas eficazes para educar seu público, estabelecendo sua marca como uma fonte confiável de informação e um parceiro valioso.

UTILIZANDO FEEDBACK E TESTEMUNHOS

Compartilhar histórias de sucesso e testemunhos de clientes satisfeitos pode ser uma maneira sutil de vender seu produto ou serviço, permitindo que as experiências de outros falem pela qualidade e eficácia da sua oferta. Isso não só demonstra o valor do que você está oferecendo, mas também reduz a percepção de risco por parte do cliente.

OFERECENDO EXPERIÊNCIAS GRATUITAS OU DEMONSTRAÇÃO

Permitir que potenciais clientes experimentem seu produto ou serviço sem compromisso pode ser uma forma eficaz de vender sem pressão. Seja oferecendo uma versão de teste, amostras grátis ou uma demonstração, você dá ao cliente a chance de ver o valor da sua oferta por si mesmos.

ESCUTANDO E ADAPTANDO

Esteja atento aos sinais do cliente e esteja pronto para adaptar sua abordagem. Se um potencial cliente parece não estar interessado ou pronto para comprar, não force a venda. Em vez disso, pergunte como você pode ser útil de outras maneiras ou se há um momento melhor para retomar a conversa.

SENDO TRANSPARENTE

A transparência sobre preços, funcionalidades e quaisquer limitações do seu produto ou serviço pode reforçar a confiança do cliente e demonstrar integridade. Clientes valorizam a honestidade e são mais propensos a fazer negócios com empresas que os tratam com respeito e abertura.

Vender sem vender é sobre criar valor, estabelecer confiança e cultivar relacionamentos. Ao focar em entender e atender às necessidades dos seus clientes, você não apenas melhora a experiência de compra para eles, mas também estabelece as bases para o sucesso a longo prazo do seu negócio.

Avançando, o próximo capítulo, **NEGOCIAÇÃO E FECHAMENTO DE VENDAS**, mergulhará nas técnicas e estratégias para efetivamente negociar e fechar vendas, assegurando que você possa converter prospectos em clientes pagantes de maneira eficiente e ética. Prepare-se para aprimorar suas habilidades de negociação e fechamento, crucial para qualquer profissional de vendas.

NEGOCIAÇÃO E FECHAMENTO DE VENDAS

A fase final do processo de vendas, a negociação e o fechamento, é onde todas as suas habilidades e esforços anteriores são postos à prova. Este capítulo se concentra em estratégias eficazes para negociar termos favoráveis e fechar vendas de maneira eficiente e ética, garantindo a satisfação do cliente e a formação de uma base sólida para relacionamentos duradouros.

ESTABELECENDO CONFIANÇA E CREDIBILIDADE

O sucesso na negociação começa bem antes da discussão de termos específicos. Ao longo de todo o processo de vendas, é crucial construir confiança e estabelecer sua credibilidade. Isso é alcançado através da compreensão profunda das necessidades do cliente, comunicação transparente e demonstração consistente do valor que sua oferta traz.

COMPREENDENDO AS NECESSIDADES DO CLIENTE

Uma negociação eficaz requer uma compreensão clara das prioridades e limitações do cliente. Antes de entrar na negociação, certifique-se de conhecer seus objetivos, o que eles valorizam mais em sua oferta e quais são seus pontos de pressão. Isso permite adaptar sua proposta de maneira que alinhe os benefícios do seu produto ou serviço com as necessidades específicas do cliente.

TÉCNICAS DE NEGOCIAÇÃO

- **Escute mais, fale menos:** A capacidade de ouvir ativamente durante uma negociação é mais valiosa do que a habilidade de falar persuasivamente. Ao escutar, você pode identificar os verdadeiros interesses do cliente e adaptar sua proposta para atender a esses interesses.

- **Crie opções de ganhos mútuos:** Procure maneiras de expandir o 'bolo' em vez de apenas dividir o que está na mesa. Isso pode envolver oferecer soluções criativas que atendam às necessidades do cliente enquanto protegem seus interesses.

- **Esteja preparado para fazer concessões:** Saiba antecipadamente quais aspectos da sua oferta são negociáveis e até onde você pode ir. Oferecer concessões estratégicas pode ajudar a facilitar um acordo, desde que não comprometam o valor central do que você está oferecendo.

FECHANDO A VENDA

O fechamento da venda é tanto sobre timing quanto sobre técnica. Identifique sinais de que o cliente está pronto para comprar, como perguntas específicas sobre preços ou implementação, e esteja preparado para oferecer um claro chamado à ação.

- **Sumarize os benefícios:** Reitere o valor que sua solução oferece, resumindo os principais benefícios e como eles atendem às necessidades identificadas do cliente.

- **Resolva as últimas objeções:** Antes de finalizar a venda, certifique-se de abordar e resolver quaisquer objeções remanescentes que o cliente possa ter.

- **Proponha o próximo passo:** Seja específico sobre o que acontece a seguir, guiando o cliente através dos passos finais do processo de compra.

PÓS-VENDA

O processo de venda não termina com a assinatura do contrato. O acompanhamento pós-venda é crucial para garantir a satisfação do cliente, resolver quaisquer problemas que surjam e estabelecer as bases para vendas futuras ou upselling. Mantenha linhas de comunicação abertas e verifique regularmente como o cliente está se saindo com sua solução.

A negociação e o fechamento de vendas requerem uma combinação de preparação, compreensão das necessidades do cliente, habilidades de comunicação e timing. Ao abordar esta fase final do processo de vendas com empatia, ética e foco na criação de valor, você pode fechar mais vendas e construir relacionamentos duradouros com seus clientes.

Avançando, o próximo capítulo, **AUTOCUIDADO E GESTÃO DO ESTRESSE EM VENDAS**, destacará a importância de manter o bem-estar pessoal no ambiente de vendas de alta pressão, oferecendo estratégias para gerenciar o estresse e manter a produtividade. Prepare-se para descobrir como equilibrar sucesso nas vendas com saúde e satisfação pessoal.

AUTOCUIDADO E GESTÃO DO ESTRESSE EM VENDAS

A carreira em vendas, embora recompensadora, pode ser fonte de significativo estresse devido às pressões constantes de metas, rejeição frequente e a necessidade de estar sempre desempenhando no seu melhor. Este capítulo aborda a importância do autocuidado e da gestão do estresse, oferecendo estratégias práticas para que profissionais de vendas mantenham seu bem-estar físico e mental, garantindo não apenas o sucesso nas vendas, mas também a saúde e satisfação pessoal.

RECONHECENDO O ESTRESSE

O primeiro passo para gerenciar o estresse é reconhecê-lo. Isso pode se manifestar de várias formas, incluindo cansaço, irritabilidade, ansiedade, dificuldades de concentração, entre outros. Aceitar que o estresse faz parte da vida e da carreira em vendas permite que você adote uma abordagem proativa para gerenciá-lo.

ESTRATÉGIAS DE AUTOCUIDADO

- **Exercício regular:** A atividade física é uma maneira eficaz de reduzir o estresse. Encontre uma forma de exercício que você goste, seja correr, yoga ou ciclismo, e incorpore-a regularmente à sua rotina.

- **Alimentação saudável:** Uma dieta equilibrada pode influenciar positivamente sua energia e seu humor. Priorize alimentos ricos em nutrientes e mantenha-se hidratado.

- **Sono de qualidade:** Garantir uma boa noite de sono é crucial para o gerenciamento do estresse. Estabeleça uma rotina relaxante antes de dormir e tente manter um horário consistente para ir para a cama e acordar.

TÉCNICAS DE GESTÃO DO ESTRESSE

- **Meditação e mindfulness:** Práticas de meditação e mindfulness podem ajudar a acalmar a mente e reduzir o estresse. Mesmo alguns minutos por dia podem fazer uma diferença significativa.

- Tempo para hobbies e interesses: Dedicar tempo a atividades que você ama fora do trabalho pode ajudar a descomprimir e manter o equilíbrio entre vida profissional e pessoal.

- Rede de suporte: Ter uma rede de suporte, seja de colegas, amigos ou familiares, é essencial. Compartilhar experiências e desafios pode proporcionar alívio e novas perspectivas.

ESTABELECENDO LIMITES

Aprender a estabelecer limites saudáveis entre o trabalho e a vida pessoal é fundamental para a gestão do estresse. Isso pode incluir definir horários específicos para verificar e-mails de trabalho, dizer não a demandas irrealistas e assegurar tempo suficiente para descanso e lazer.

REFLEXÃO E AJUSTE

Permita-se momentos regulares de reflexão sobre seu bem-estar e progresso nas estratégias de autocuidado. Seja gentil consigo mesmo e reconheça que a gestão do estresse é um processo contínuo. Esteja aberto a ajustar suas estratégias conforme necessário para encontrar o que funciona melhor para você.

Cuidar de si mesmo é essencial para manter a produtividade e a satisfação em uma carreira em vendas. Adotando estratégias de autocuidado e gestão do estresse, você pode enfrentar os desafios inerentes à profissão de forma mais eficaz, garantindo não apenas o sucesso nas vendas, mas também uma vida mais equilibrada e gratificante.

Prosseguindo, o próximo e último capítulo, **PLANO DE AÇÃO DE 30 DIAS PARA PROSPECÇÃO ATIVA**, fornecerá um guia passo a passo para colocar em prática as estratégias e insights discutidos ao longo do livro, ajudando você a começar a construir sua base de clientes agora. Prepare-se para traçar um caminho claro em direção ao sucesso na prospecção.

PLANO DE AÇÃO DE 30 DIAS PARA PROSPECÇÃO ATIVA

Este capítulo final fornece um plano de ação concreto e estruturado para os próximos 30 dias, projetado para ajudá-lo a implementar as estratégias de prospecção ativa discutidas ao longo deste livro. Seguindo este guia passo a passo, você poderá começar a construir e expandir sua base de clientes de maneira eficaz e sistemática.

DIA 1-5: PREPARAÇÃO E PLANEJAMENTO

- **Dia 1:** Revise e defina seus objetivos de prospecção. Quais são suas metas de vendas para os próximos 30 dias? Seja específico e mensurável.

- **Dia 2:** Realize uma pesquisa de mercado e identifique seu público-alvo. Quem são seus clientes ideais? Quais são suas necessidades e pontos de dor?

- **Dia 3:** Desenvolva sua proposta de valor. Por que clientes potenciais deveriam escolher você? Como você pode solucionar os problemas deles de maneira única?

- **Dia 4:** Prepare seu material de prospecção. Isso pode incluir scripts de chamada fria, templates de e-mail, e conteúdo educativo ou promocional.

- **Dia 5:** Organize suas ferramentas e recursos. Certifique-se de que seu CRM está atualizado, configure qualquer software de automação necessário, e planeje sua rotina diária de prospecção.

DIA 6-10: IMPLEMENTAÇÃO INICIAL

- **Dia 6-7:** Inicie atividades de chamada fria com base na sua pesquisa e preparação. Foque em escutar ativamente e adaptar sua abordagem conforme necessário.

- **Dia 8:** Envie seus primeiros lotes de e-mails de prospecção. Utilize os templates preparados, mas personalize cada mensagem para o destinatário.

- **Dia 9:** Engaje com clientes potenciais nas redes sociais. Comente publicações relevantes, participe de grupos do seu setor e compartilhe conteúdo valioso.

- **Dia 10:** Avalie e ajuste suas estratégias de prospecção. O que funcionou bem? O que pode ser melhorado?

DIA 11-20: EXPANSÃO E OTIMIZAÇÃO

- **Dia 11-15:** Continue com as atividades de prospecção, aumentando gradualmente o volume conforme você se torna mais confortável e eficiente em suas abordagens.

- **Dia 16:** Implemente uma estratégia de conteúdo focada na geração de leads. Isso pode incluir postar um blog informativo, lançar um webinar ou publicar um estudo de caso.

- **Dia 17-18:** Explore novos canais de prospecção. Isso pode envolver parcerias com influenciadores, participação em eventos virtuais, ou campanhas de anúncios pagos.

- **Dia 19-20:** Realize follow-ups estratégicos. Utilize insights de interações anteriores para personalizar suas mensagens e ofertas.

DIA 21-30: AVALIAÇÃO E AJUSTE CONTÍNUO

- **Dia 21-25:** Mantenha um ritmo constante de atividades de prospecção, incorporando feedback e aprendizados de seus esforços anteriores.

- **Dia 26:** Colete e analise dados. Revise os KPIs de prospecção estabelecidos inicialmente e avalie seu desempenho.

- **Dia 27-28:** Faça ajustes baseados em sua análise. Refine suas estratégias, mensagens e abordagens conforme necessário.

- **Dia 29:** Planeje os próximos passos. Com base em seu

progresso, estabeleça objetivos para o próximo mês.

- Dia 30: Reserve um tempo para reflexão e autocuidado. Reconheça seus esforços e sucessos, e assegure-se de cuidar de sua saúde mental e física.

Este plano de ação de 30 dias é um ponto de partida para você implementar e aprimorar suas estratégias de prospecção ativa. Lembre-se de que a prospecção é um processo contínuo que requer adaptação, aprendizado e persistência. Ao seguir este guia, você estará bem equipado para construir uma base sólida de clientes e impulsionar o crescimento do seu negócio.

Ao virarmos a última página desta jornada juntos, espero sinceramente que os aprendizados compartilhados aqui tenham tocado seu coração e despertado novas perspectivas. Se este livro lhe trouxe algum valor, peço gentilmente que dedique alguns momentos para deixar sua avaliação na Amazon. Suas palavras não apenas me ajudam a crescer e aprimorar minha arte, mas também guiam outros leitores em suas buscas por conhecimento e inspiração. Sua opinião é um presente valioso, tanto para mim quanto para a comunidade de leitores em busca de histórias que transformam. Agradeço de coração por compartilhar esta jornada comigo e espero que possamos nos encontrar novamente nas páginas de uma nova aventura.

REGINALDO OSNILDO

Olá, sou Reginaldo Osnildo, autor e inovador nas áreas de vendas, tecnologia, e estratégias de comunicação. Minha experiência abrange desde o ambiente acadêmico, como professor e pesquisador na Universidade do Sul de Santa Catarina, até a prática como estrategista no Grupo Catarinense de Rádios. Com um doutorado em narrativas de vendas e convergência digital, e um mestrado em storytelling e imaginário social, eu trago para meus leitores uma fusão única entre teoria e prática. Meu objetivo é fornecer conhecimento em uma linguagem simples, prática e didática, incentivando a aplicação direta na vida pessoal e profissional.

Atenciosamente

Prof. Dr. Reginaldo Osnildo

+55 48 991913865

reginaldoosnildo@gmail.com

www.ingramcontent.com/pod-product-compliance
Lightning Source LLC
Chambersburg PA
CBHW050323230526
45471CB00005B/2330